Students and External Readers	Staff & Research Students
DATE DUE FOR RETURN	**DATE OF ISSUE**
	25 JUN 2000 600
	N.B. All books must be returned for the Annual Inspection in June

Any book which you borrow remains your responsibility until the loan slip is cancelled

HIGH-LEVEL MANPOWER IN IRAN

HIGH-LEVEL MANPOWER IN IRAN

From Hidden Conflict to Crisis

Gail Cook Johnson

PRAEGER

PRAEGER SPECIAL STUDIES • PRAEGER SCIENTIFIC

Library of Congress Cataloging in Publication Data

Johnson, Gail Cook.
  Failure of industrialization under the Shah.

  Bibliography: p.
  Includes index.
  1. Iran--Industries.   2. Elite (Social sciences)
--Iran.   3. Entrepreneur.   I. Title.
HC475.J64   338'.0955   79-21419

ISBN 0-03-053366-X

Published in 1980 by Praeger Publishers
CBS Educational and Professional Publishing
A Division of CBS, Inc.
521 Fifth Avenue, New York, New York 10017 U.S.A.

© 1980 by Praeger Publishers

0123456789   038   987654321

Printed in the United States of America

To My Parents,
Preston Reid Cook and Barbara Marie Cook

PREFACE

The recent overthrow of the Shah of Iran has distressed the Western world, which is so dependent upon Iranian oil supplies. Indeed, the experience has underscored the potential instability of other oil-exporting nations. This book explains some of the underlying causes that precipitated the Iranian revolution from the perspective of Iran's high-level manpower.

The findings presented here follow from a year and half spent in Iran researching manpower problems. The discussion takes an interdisciplinary approach and stresses the interplay of economic and sociopolitical factors within the context of the labor market and organizational development.

The encouragement and support that I have received from many persons have made this book possible. In particular, Charles A. Myers, professor emeritus at the Sloan School of Management, provided wise instruction and transmitted to me the confidence with which to conduct my own investigations. His continuing interest has been a welcome source of inspiration. Ken Mericle of Sloan and Michael Piore of the economics department at the Massachusetts Institute of Technology also imparted invaluable intellectual guidance.

The Canada Council provided financial assistance during the course of this research. Pat Gardner patiently helped in the preparation of the final manuscript.

I am also indebted to the assistance I received from persons in Iran. The Statistical Centre of Iran provided support facilities and, in many cases, the necessary letters of introduction to executives in both the public and private sectors. The support of Firouz Tofigh, past director of the center, is gratefully acknowledged. Fereshteh Amirfaryar was particularly helpful in conducting interviews and searching for pertinent literature. Many others in Iran were very generous with their time and graciously consented to answer detailed interview questions. These persons must remain anonymous in accordance with their wishes. However, without them, this study would not have progressed beyond the drawing board. The sincere concern that many of these persons share for their country inevitably will be of great assistance to Iran.

Finally, I thank my husband Neil Alexander Johnson. His insightful comments and understanding have been of great assistance.

CONTENTS

LIST OF TABLES AND FIGURES

HIGH-LEVEL
MANPOWER
IN IRAN

1

INTRODUCTION

The dramatic rise in oil prices at the end of 1973 propelled Iran onto a path of accelerating growth sustained by burgeoning oil revenues. To the outside observer, Iran's future held great promise for a stable regime committed to the rapid modernization of Iranian society. The control over the billions in oil revenues enabled the Shah to establish Iran in a preeminent role of regional leader in both military and economic spheres. Unlike Saudi Arabia, Iran's population of 33 million provided the manpower base and domestic market capable of absorbing the massive economic stimulus.

In this almost euphoric environment, traditional divisions within the Iranian society were concealed, and barriers to rapid economic and social development were perceived as both minor and transitory. The ambitious development plans envisaged the transformation of Iranian society with over 50 percent illiteracy in 1970 to a modern industrial state within two decades. This was not to be. Civil disruptions that began in 1978 caused the overthrow of the Shah in early 1979. The outpouring of violent protest laid bare the profound divisions within Iranian society so successfully concealed through censorship and government control.

It became apparent that the industrialization plan embarked upon in 1974 could not fulfill the high expectations for economic and social gain that it had fostered among the diverse social groups in Iran. The lack of timely and concerted efforts in some sectors undermined the development of essential linkages among sectors of the economy and resulted in a deterioration in relative economic positions of some groups, most notably those in the rural parts of the country. Even in the most heavily stressed sectors, such as manufacturing, the anticipated levels of performance were not forthcoming. Political repression, combined with the economic deprivation of politically and economically weak groups, formed the basis of the growing frustration of Iranians, which finally exploded in 1979.

Perhaps the most shocking aspect of the revolution in Iran was the absence of middle-class support for the Shah's regime, despite the fact that they appeared to have benefited the most from the Shah's policies. The explanation for this phenomenon lies in the recognition that the process of modernization and industrial expansion had been retarded by institutional barriers and did not meet the expectations of the growing number of educated Iranians. These barriers caused opportunities for those engaged in high-level occupations to become more limited over time.

Induced by the failure of industrialization, the social revolution therefore was founded upon economic disillusionment of both the middle and working classes. The strikes that plagued the latter period of the Shah's regime included not only the traditional working class but also large numbers of high-level manpower, and were indicative of the pervasive malaise within the work force.

The primary thrust of the following analysis is to indicate why government policies in the private sector failed to cope with the demands of industrialization and why firms were unable to integrate effectively high-level manpower (HLM) into the economic system. Under the rapid pace of industrial expansion set by the development plans of 1974, the demand for HLM exceeded its supply. The adaptation to this excess demand of HLM within institutions designed to forward the modernization effort is of crucial importance. A major concern of this study therefore is with the utilization of HLM and the critical role played by institutional processes, that is, the mechanisms of the internal labor market in adjusting to the rapidly changing economic environment of Iran.

In order to gain a better insight into the problems confronting HLM and the behavior of private sector firms, case studies were conducted in Tehran during the spring and summer of 1976. Employers were interviewed to obtain information on personnel policies and organization structures. HLM employees were requested to provide information on career and demographic characteristics.

The results of the analysis concentrate upon five large manufacturing firms that employed over 1,000 employees.* These firms, which were chosen provide good examples of the role played by imported technology in Iranian industrialization and represent situations where independence from traditional behavioral patterns in internal labor market arrangements was potentially possible. The problems facing these firms were typical of large, private sector institutions in Iran.

In addition to a detailed examination of these private firms, specific comparisons to organizations in the government sector are made. This part of the

---

*While five is a small number, the total number of establishments employing over 1,000 employees was also very small. Off-the-record discussions with other industrialists were had in the course of the author's stay in Iran and indicated that the institutional problems were similar to those evaluated here.

analysis underscores the meaningful interconnections that existed between the Iranian private and public domains.

In the context of this analysis, HLM is defined by occupation rather than education.* Job titles and job descriptions that indicated the employee performed job duties of a professional, technical, managerial, or supervisory nature were included as HLM occupations. As such, the definition encompasses upper, middle, and lower managerial echelons, as well as middle- and upper-level professionals and technicians employed in Iranian organizations.[1]

HLM, so defined, forms an integral part of the emerging middle class, which is distinct from the traditional bourgeoisie centered in the bazaar. The position of HLM in the Iranian social structure is of particular significance. As a group, they seemingly had a great deal to gain from the modernization effort that generated excess demands for their skills and had the potential for opening up new avenues for social mobility. The expectations of social and economic improvement of HLM and the opportunities presented to them in reality caused a critical expectations gap.

Studies of those classes above and below this middle HLM group do not offer an enlightening analysis of the impact of specific institutional factors upon economic opportunity. Success among the elite, who included the owner-managers of large manufacturing establishments and top political advisers, was influenced by the degree to which they were in direct favor with the Shah. As such, their behavior was affected by higher political intrigues. For this book, they are only of concern because they were the chief designers of the organizational dynamics that affected the economic opportunies of HLM and other groups.

Among the industrial working class, many other factors impinged upon manpower utilization at the corporate level. In order to deal aptly with the problems of blue-collar workers, for example, questions concerning elementary literacy, the transition from rural to urban environment, and the introduction to the worker of the most basic realities of industrial life become of crucial importance. Due to the enormity of these adjustment problems from the supply side, the specific influence of individual organizations is almost impossible to

---

*High-level manpower traditionally has been defined as those persons holding at least one university degree. However, such a definition, while permitting comparison among persons of equal educational qualifications, does not capture those who may occupy high-level job positions but possess no degree. The omission of such persons in a study concerning a developing country such as Iran can be serious. Higher education for a significant number of individuals had only been offered very recently in Iran. One could not assume at the outset of a study that the vast majority of the people occupying high-level positions have university degrees, particularly older employees. The employment of persons without degrees in such positions, moreover, could represent an important aspect of high-level manpower utilization in Iran.

isolate and analyze. Members of the HLM group, on the other hand, have already accepted many of the facts of industrialization. Thus examination of HLM presents the researcher with a clearer view of manpower utilization problems fostered solely by organizational processes.

The basic assumption upon which this book is based is that internal organizational arrangements are responses to economic circumstances that create a need for the development of some order within an institution. However, the specific features of this resulting order are determined through the resolution of power relationships among the actors of the marketplace: the government, the employer, and the employee.

That organizational processes are influenced by the economic, social, and political environment of the country is, of course, not a new concept. But that power relationships ultimately determine organizational reactions to economic circumstances means that job placement, promotion, and other aspects of manpower utilization can be governed by traditions or customs that are largely independent of economic decisions of immediate concern.[2] In other words, anachronistic organizational arrangements can persist, at least in the short run, because the actors in the marketplace, maintaining the balance of power, have motivations to resist change.

This implies that private sector organizations may fail to adapt to the changing external environment and may be incapable of providing structure that effectively utilizes manpower. As a result, internal labor markets may stagnate so that HLM lacks both the incentives or upgrading of skills required to meet challenges to organizations. As long as the economy experiences rapid growth and competition is limited or nonexistent, organizations can continue without crisis. But what happens when there is a deterioration in the economic environment and organizations must cope with adversity? What factors prove to be of critical importance in retarding organizational adaptation and contribute to the instability of the manpower system in the private sector?

In order to answer these questions, one must recognize that the Shah held the balance of power over all other groups, and this had crucial import for the shape of internal labor markets. Iran, under the Shah, was unusual in that it was controlled by one of the few operative monarchies in the world. He dominated the behavior of employers through political channels that rewarded and punished entrepreneurs accordingly. Many of the economic constraints faced by employers were indeed mediated by the industrialization plan that dictated the number and location of firms in any one industry, controlled access to available supply facilities, and provided development incentives. The plan provided the greatest inducements for capital-intensive approaches to be used in industry. Employees, the third actor in the marketplace, were either organized, as in the case of the industrial working class, under the auspices of the government, or, in the case of HLM, had no central organized voice. Power within this latter group rested solely within individual bargaining positions with each employer.

The lack of diffusion of power and economic decision making, which stemmed from the concentration of power in Iran, lent itself to instability. This same phenomenon existed within organizations and left them equally incapable of coping with the disintegration of Iran's political and economic system. In order to understand the failure of industrialization in Iran, one must therefore examine not only the macroshocks to the Iranian economy but also the failure within firms to manage change effectively. The sociopolitical environment created a high degree of uncertainty for entrepreneurs that limited their commitment to long-term organizational goals. The economic environment created naturally high turnover thresholds within organizations and consequently a lack of incentive to invest in manpower development. Moreover, the high rate of inflation prevented the effective structuring of monetary incentives. In total, the external factors helped to preserve traditional values that respected personal relationships more than demonstrated ability.

Within the organization, traditionalism largely governed initial and subsequent job placements. After personal connections, foreign university education, regardless of the field of specialization, was most valued. The attainment of such education, in turn, was largely influenced by family background. In general, organization structures were governed by the avilability of friends and relatives to fill positions and not by economic requirements. Organization processes were very informal.

Similar behavior existed within government organizations despite the fact that these appeared to have the trappings of a formalized personnel system. The comparison between private and public sector institutions indicates the extent to which the external environment impinged upon internal working relationships. Civil servants were equally motivated to protect their positions from the onslaught of political change, as were entrepreneurs desirous to combat the unstable environment through short-term gain. The style of administration that was encouraged by the Shah within his civil service appeared to be the prototype for private sector organizations.

In one private Iranian organization some formal personnel policies were being developed to help identify ability within the organization. In this case, the changes were the result of organizational aging and the deaths of the original founders of the firm. In a foreign-managed firm, well-developed personnel policies did exist. However, in this case, the orderly advancement of capable Iranian personnel stopped short of the top decision-making positions.

Certain career profiles were noted to characterize HLM on the basis of the quality or "intimacy" of their connections with the industrial elite and the quality of their education. Ironically, the Iranian-educated university graduates who came from lower- and middle-class family backgrounds and who gained the most by the universalization of higher education in Iran under the Shah were most limited in their career options. They were confined to low-level managerial positions with limited opportunity for either intra- or interorganizational mobility. The conflicting pressures on HLM within both the public and private sectors inhibited organizational development and limited the integration of HLM in Iran's industrial systems.

The results of the analysis indicate that social and economic development in Iran was highly dependent upon the continuing and stable flow of oil revenues. Despite some signs of change which had been fostered by the push of industrialization, dependency upon oil revenues nonetheless remained the essential cornerstone to the industrial strategy. The fluctuation in Iran's oil revenues as a result of the undercutting of prices by OPEC (Organization of Petroleum Exporting Countries) members dealt the final blow to industrialization plans devised in 1974 and ultimately to the Shah's regime.

The future of Iran under the present Islamic republic is impossible to predict. However, given that industrialization in the private sector has been placed in turmoil by political events, and that there is an absence of foreigners to maintain the large amounts of imported technology installed in Iran, prospects for industrialization are very limited in the short run. From the social perspective, it is not clear that the revolution has lowered economic expectations, so that a slower pace of industrial development may be accepted, or that, in the final analysis, the Khomeini elite, which has supplanted that which existed under the Shah, will succeed in resolving old social inequities without creating new, but equally volatile, imbalances.

Whereas the conclusions of this book relate specifically to Iran, they also have pertinence for other developing nations. Insight into questions concerning the debate of balanced versus unbalanced growth, the processes of organizational change, and the role of technology is offered. For example, a great deal of useful research has been directed toward the study of why developing nations choose a particular technology and the consequences of that choice in terms of the country's ability to produce desired levels of output. Certainly, the relatively high level of wages in Iran compared to that of its eastern neighbors and Iran's desire, and in some sectors, need, to be competitive with developed countries, as well as other factors, have contributed to capital-intensive choices of technology in Iran.

But not enough has been stated about the *social* significance of technological choice vis-a-vis its potential impact upon manpower utilization. One reason why Iranian-educated HLM, for instance, were unable to succeed within modern industrial firms was that the higher educational system in Iran could not advance sufficiently to produce manpower qualified to meet the demands of foreign technology. This is despite the fact that persons gaining entrance to Iranian universities since the institution of universal entrance examinations were within the top 15 percent of the student population. The mismatching of educational opportunities with those offered in the labor market served as a catalyst for discontent and in part had its foundations in technological constraints.

Another conclusion indicated by this study is that not only must industrial strategies attempt to accommodate changes in social policy, such as in educa-tion, but that the pace of economic development must not overstrain the so-ciety's capacity to adapt culturally and psychologically to the demands of modernization. The pressures of industrialization undoubtedly can generate a healthy climate for social change. However, as the rate of expansion increases, capacities for social change can be exceeded. The examination of organizations in Iran revealed how traditional social values are incompatible with ambitious industrialization plans.

Most studies of HLM in developing nations have been within the frame-work of traditional economic analysis.[3] By assuming an optimal relationship between human resource development and economic development, manpower planners have produced quantitative models designed to forecast the number of persons at various educational levels needed to provide for a certain level of out-put, given the level of technology. The optimization approach has suffered from a lack of data and in particular from the fact that little is known about the rela-tionship between education and occupation, although most certainly it is not an optimal one.[4]

Microstudies can aid manpower planners in formulating policies by pro-viding a better understanding of the relationship between supply of manpower and its demand. For this reason, a 1971 conference of the Organization for Eco-nomic Cooperation and Development made the following recommendation:

> that attempts at quantitative forecasting should be completed by qualitative analyses, both more delicate and less far-reaching; these analyses themselves should take account of the work done in psychology and sociology. . . .[5]

Regrettably, microstudies focused upon HLM are very few in developing nations and are not easily accessible. Moreover, these tend to stress only the supply side of the equation.[6]

This study is divided into two parts. The first part examines the impact of the economic and sociopolitical environment upon internal organizational arrangements in Chapters 2 and 3, respectively. In the second part, organiza-tional policies that affect the utilization of HLM are outlined in Chapter 4 and the specific aspects of HLM careers using the employee data gathered for this study are analyzed in Chapter 5. Finally, Chapter 6 summarizes results, and their significance with respect to recent occurrences in Iran, as well as in other developing nations.

NOTES

1. A job, in short, was categorized as a HLM position if it fell into the broad cate-gories of "professional, technical, and related workers" and "administrative and managerial

workers"; the major groups of "clerical supervisors" and "government executive officials" under the broad category of "clerical and related workers"; and "managers" and "sales supervisors" under the broad category of "sales workers" as outlined by the International Labor Office, *International Standard Classification of Occupations*, rev. ed. (Geneva, 1975).

2. For a discussion of such an approach as applied to the United States with emphasis upon blue-collar workers, see Peter B. Doeringer and Michael J. Piore, *Internal Labor Markets and Manpower Analysis* (Lexington, Mass.: Heath, 1971).

3. For example, see I. Adelman and E. Thorbecke, eds., *The Theory and Design of Economic Development* (Baltimore: Johns Hopkins Press, 1966); and H. B. Chenery, ed., *Studies in Development Planning* (Cambridge, Mass.: Harvard University Press, 1971).

4. For insight into this question, see M. Blaug, M. Peston, and A. Ziderman, *The Utilisation of Educated Manpower in Industry: A Preliminary Report* (London: Oliver and Boyd, 1967). Two publications have followed from this preliminary study. See M. Blaug, "The Correlation Between Education and Earnings: What Does It Signify?" *Higher Education*, 3 (1973) (Winter, 1972). 53–76; and P. R. G. Layard, J. D. Sargan, M. E. Ager, and D. J. Jones, *Qualified Manpower and Economic Performance* (London: Allen Lane, Penguin Press, 1971).

5. Organization for Economic Cooperation and Development, *The Utilization of Highly Qualified Manpower: Venice Conference, 25th–27th October, 1971* (Paris, 1973), p. 14.

6. T. Hillard Cox directed a survey of high-level manpower in Iran (now out-of-date) and was concerned solely with educational planning: "High-Level Manpower Development in Iran," *Manpower Advisor* (Tehran: Governmental Affairs Institute, 1960), mimeographed. For surveys for highly qualified manpower in a developing nation context, see also S. K. Basu, G. Ghosh, and R. N. Banerjee, *Labour Market Behaviour in a Developing Economy* (New Delhi: New Age Publishers, 1969); and Madras State Employment Informtion Unit, *Short-term Study of the Utilisation Pattern of Educated Persons Produced During the Third Plan Period in Madras State* (Madras, 1968).

I

FOUNDATIONS FOR INTERNAL LABOR MARKETS IN IRAN

2

ECONOMIC DEVELOPMENT AND
HIGH-LEVEL MANPOWER

The high oil price increases instituted by OPEC in December 1973 quadrupled Iranian oil revenues in a very short period of time. This action embarked Iran upon an unprecedented and ambitious development program that was envisioned by the Shah to make Iran a leading developed nation by 1982/83.[1] While few investors took seriously these lofty development goals, Iran's newly gained financial status, which provided much needed foreign exchange, enhanced Iran's borrowing ability from foreign money markets, and financed large government expenditures that directly or indirectly stimulated domestic demand for modern industrial products, fostered enough confidence in the Iranian economy to attract large amounts of direct foreign investment between 1974 and 1976. Undoubtedly, these investors were also encouraged by what appeared to be the relative political stability of the Pahlavi dynasty since the fall of Mohammed Mossadegh in 1953. This acceleration of economic development severely overburdened Iran's scarcest resource—HLM.

The pace of industrialization could not be sustained. By the end of the 1976/77 fiscal year, Iran showed a government deficit for the first time since 1973 and the increase in oil revenues.[2] Iranian planning authorities also had come to the decision that many of the investment projects slated to begin during the Fifth Plan (1973-78) would have to be postponed at least until the Sixth Plan. Only projects already under way were scheduled to be completed.[3] By 1979, moreover, after almost a year of civil disruptions, the political stability of the Pahlavi dynasty became a broken myth.

The attempts at rapid industrialization in Iran, particularly since 1973, and the attendant misfortunes created the context surrounding the development of institutional policies in the nation. These have affected the recruitment, placement, and rules of work (in short, the internal labor market) for high-level manpower. As such, the details of industrialization to be discussed in this chapter and the sociopolitical environment (discussed in Chapter 3) that have mediated the process deserve examination.[4]

Many of the specifics of the Iranian case are naturally unique. Indeed, the forces that have conspired to bring about the political turmoil of 1978–79 and the consequent full stop of industrialization plans, at least temporarily, is an extreme occurrence. Nonetheless, many of the failures of economic policy in Iran offer valuable lessons to other developing countries that are struggling to make the social and economic transition to a developed nation. This is particularly pertinent for some of the OPEC nations that have similarly reaped large foreign exchange reserves from the oil price increases at the end of 1973.[5]

OVERVIEW OF ECONOMIC DEVELOPMENT

The highly erratic trend of economic performance in Iran from 1971 to March 1978 is evidenced by the gross domestic product (GDP) figures displayed in Table 2.1. While the growth rates of nominal GDP have at least been impressively high, though fluctuating, during the period, the growth of GDP at 1975 prices is truly alarming. By 1977/78, the economy had become so overheated, as witnessed by high rates of inflation, that real growth was negative.

The unbalanced nature of Iranian economic development accounts for these trends. Writing of economic policy in 1971, Jahangir Amuzegar and Ali Fekrat stated:

> The planners seem to have felt that, in industry, the main bottle-necks that determine the rate of output expansion . . . are essentially specialized labor and capital equipment. In agriculture, on the other hand, the major obstacle to expansion has appeared to be mostly organizational and structural. . . . The solutions of these problems, in the planners' opinion, have apparently called for essentially different talents and capabilities. For one thing, they argue, the rectification of the agricultural constraints does not require heavy outlays of foreign exchange. . . . For another, it does not call forth the many specialized human resources claimed by industry.[6]

Thus, by the advent of the Fifth Plan (1973–78) and its revision in August 1974, which used the newly established oil wealth to double government expenditures and projected growth rates, the much greater priority given to the development of modern industry over the agricultural sector was already well established.[7]

This has meant that the land reform laws, first enacted in 1962 to address the structural problems in the agricultural sector, have been far from successful.[8] The actual growth in agriculture had fallen to an estimated 2.5 percent per year,[9] well below the increase in demand for foodstuffs of 12 percent a year.[10] As a result, in 1978, Iran had to import approximately $2 billion worth of

TABLE 2.1

Gross Domestic Product in Iran: Levels and Rates of Growth, 1971/72 to 1977/78*

Levels

	Year						
	1971/72	1972/73	1973/74	1974/75	1975/76	1976/77	1977/78
(billions of rials)							
GDP at market prices	1,014.3	1,268.4	1,868.6	3,137.0	3,561.1	4,606.6	5,393.3
GDP at 1975 prices	2,458.4	2,873.4	3,210.7	3,461.1	3,561.1	3,940.9	3,859.4

Rates of Growth

	Year					
	1972/73	1973/74	1974/75	1975/76	1976/77	1977/78
(percent)						
GDP at market prices	25.1	47.3	67.9	13.5	29.4	17.1
GDP at 1975 prices	16.9	11.7	7.8	2.9	10.7	(2.1)

*The Iranian year begins March 21.
Source: International Monetary Fund, *International Financial Statistics*, January 1979.

foodstuffs.[11] A decade ago, the nation was a net exporter of food.

The poor performance in the agricultural sector has prevented it from either becoming an expanding market for the output of the industrial sector, both for consumer and capital goods, or from providing stabilizing forward linkages to the modern sector.[12] Thus the industrialization process has had to rely principally upon the increased expansion of oil revenues, revenues that were being substantially drained by the necessity for food imports.

This dependence upon oil revenues has been a chief deterrent to Iran's industrialization efforts. The high and accelerating growth rates of GDP from 1971/72 to 1974/75, for instance (see Table 2.1), may be largely attributed to the oil price increases instituted, first, by the Tehran Agreements of 1971 and, second, by OPEC in 1973. Similarly, the decline in GDP in 1975/76 and again in 1977/78 was governed by the decline in oil revenues caused, in the former year, by undercutting of oil prices in other OPEC countries and, in the latter year, by the two-tier price structure that was implemented in December 1976.[13] Iran's reliance on oil revenues, moreover, had been accelerating. "For instance, the Third Plan (1962-67) was 62 percent dependent upon oil revenues, the Fourth Plan (1968-72) 63 percent. By the time of the revision of the Fifth Plan (1973-78) following the 1973 oil price rises, the dependence had risen to over 80 percent."[14]

THE NATURE OF ECONOMIC DEVELOPMENT IN THE MODERN SECTOR

While small-scale workshops, particularly those specializing in art and handicrafts, have had a long tradition in Iran, the growth of modern industry, that is, large-scale factory production and technologically based establishments, is relatively recent. Its early beginnings, which date back to the 1920s and 1930s, were troubled by the world depression, World War II, the ensuing control by foreign powers, and the Mossadegh era. It was not until the late 1950s to 1960s that spectacular growth in Iranian industry was first witnessed.[15]

In actual size, the modern sector has never been very large. In 1967, there were only 586 firms that employed 50 or more workers. This was only 0.4 percent of the total number of industrial establishments located within urban centers where all of the modern sector has been centered.[16] This figure, a decade later, rose to 800 firms, but 72 percent of the industrial labor force were employed in units of under 10 persons. In addition, very few establishments could be considered large, that is, over 1,000 employees.[17]

Estimates of growth in the modern sector are offered by various statistical sources.* For example, gross value added in real terms in industry and mines

---

*Although, because of the weakness in statistics, it should be mentioned that the statistics offer only approximate estimates.

for the period of 1960-70 has been estimated to have increased at an average annual rate of 11.8 percent. The pace of development was accelerating during this entire period: the rates of growth being 10.2 percent in 1960/65 and 13.6 percent in 1965/70.[18] Similarly, the production index compiled by the Bank Markazi (Central Bank) indicates that industry had been growing at a rate of 16.5 percent per year from 1969/70 to 1974/75.[19]

Since 1975 and before the overthrow of the Shah's regime, the modern sector had suffered badly. Many of the optimistic production plans of the industrial firms were based upon the unrealistic assumption, which was encouraged by the government, that Iran could become a major exporter of consumer durables to Third World nations. However, rapidly rising costs, an inadequate infrastructure that caused power failures and prevented needed capital goods from arriving in time through overburdened ports, and a lack of manpower to maintain installations placed Iranian industry at a comparative disadvantage in the international market. Even supposing a steady increase in oil revenues, it was infeasible that the necessary support resources could have expanded at a rate fast enough to accommodate the modern sector's development goals.

Given the decline in oil revenues after the increase in 1973, the shelving of many development projects and the decline in subsidies to the private sector made the situation worse. Robert Graham, in fact, reported that: "A government study early in 1977 found that capacity utilization was 61 percent in textiles, 96 percent in cement, 46 percent in brick-making, 69 percent in the automotive industry (51 percent in the car industry) and 32 percent in tractors."[20]

GROWTH OF HLM EMPLOYMENT

On the manpower side of the industrialization effort, overall employment in industry expanded at a rate of 5.8 percent per year from 1965 to 1968, according to one source.[21] During the 1970s, the Bank Markazi figures showed that it increased by 7 percent a year from 1969/70 to 1974/75.[22] Regardless of the fact that these statistics are difficult to compare, they demonstrate that growth in employment has not been as spectacular as the growth in production over the same period and that the bias of growth has been clearly capital-intensive rather than employment-generating. Investment expansion has been concentrated primarily in the petrochemical and related industries, then in consumer durable industries, and only secondarily in such traditional industries as food processing, textiles, and wood finishing. This capital-intensive growth bias, however, has been complementary to the demand for HLM.

Due to the sampling and definitional problems, there are no meaningful statistics that relate specifically to the growth of HLM employment in the industrial sector.[23] Nevertheless, there is much evidence to attest to the growing importance of such manpower. Before the expansion boom in the 1970s, for example, the demand for white-collar workers in the oil industry was expanding, despite declining employment levels for the industry in general.[24] The 1969 figures on income distribution also showed that university degree holders on the average earned almost four times that of primary school leavers and five times that of illiterates. The distribution of income by occupation as found by the Ministry of Labor's manpower survey in 1969, on the other hand, stated that the average earnings of trained, specialist manpower were ten times higher than those received by unskilled workers. When hours of work were accounted for, this figure rose to fifteen times.[25]

Admittedly, there is much disparity between these figures. But in all cases these ratios are significantly higher than those in the developed economies of Europe and the United States. The worsening income distribution since that time in Iran has been partly caused by educational differences and the demand for HLM. This has led one researcher to conclude that only the provision of well-paid jobs for unskilled and uneducated labor in urban centers would help to solve the distribution problems in the short run.[26] This would suggest a more labor-intensive approach.

~~Concomitant with the growth in Iranian industry has also been the growth~~ in foreign national employment in Iran. In 1965, the number of foreigners employed did not exceed 4,000.[27] But in July 1975, over 20,000 work permits had been issued to foreign nationals.[28] This figure was estimated to reach the 60,000 mark in 1977.[29] Moreover, a breakdown of the 1975 statistics reveals that 23 percent of the foreigners were employed by the manufacturing sector, that 50.6 percent of the non-Iranians performed professional and technical jobs, and that 13.5 percent were managers and administrators.[30]

The increasing number of foreign nationals in Iran becomes a particularly telling indicator of the HLM situation when the ambivalent attitude toward foreigners during the Shah's reign is considered. The official government attitude was adequately summarized in a news bulletin from the *Iran Economic Service*:

> Because the number of foreign nationals was small in the past, the Ministry of Labor was not strict in enforcing the [work permit] law, but it intends to enforce it from 21 January, 1976. Under the law, employers who take foreign nationals without a work permit will be subject to fines and imprisonment [2 months or more]. Furthermore, more attention will be paid to applicants from the point of view of their personal conduct, political views, etc.[31]

A highly placed bureaucrat in the Ministry of Labor who was interviewed for background material in this study expressed the personal view that he resented foreigners in Iran because they seemed incapable of integrating into the society.* In a similar vein, an executive of the Iranian Management Association stated in an interview that: "Iran wishes to get away from the American managers because they, (a) do not know Farsi, (b) do not know the system for doing business in Iran, (c) do not know the laws, and (d) do not want to know any of the above."† Clearly, given these views, foreigners would not be welcome if Iranians with similar abilities could be found. Ambivalence toward foreigners turned to unmitigated resentment during the 1978-79 turmoil.

That the supply of HLM had in fact been one of the chief problems of development was well established. This position is the predominant view expressed by the Fifth Plan. In June 1975, "a survey of the press [also] showed that an average of 1,000 'situation vacant' advertisements appear daily in the press. Of these, about 40 percent are for engineers and technicians."[32]

CAUSES OF HLM SHORTAGE

The shortage of HLM is caused in part by the lack of higher education institutions in Iran. In 1975, for instance, 28,000 students passed the university entrance examinations. This figure represents only 14.7 percent of the secondary school graduates who actually wrote them.[33] More students could not be permitted to qualify for university entrance because of the limited number of available places in the universities.

Many of the students who did not qualify for the university therefore enrolled in universities abroad, providing they had the material resources to do so. In 1974-75, as many as 45,000 to 60,000 were thought to be attending universities outside Iran.[34] Moreover, due to more favorable living and working conditions abroad, the majority of these students were not expected to return to Iran. In 1966:

> It has been estimated by an Iranian government official that approximately 50 percent of the privately supported students from middle class families, 60 percent of government and foundation supported students and an equal percentage of privately supported upper-class students, and 90 percent of students who have failed academically do not return to Iran from Europe and the United States.[35]

---

*Interview with Fereydoun Nasseri, Deputy Minister Ministry of Labor and Social Affairs on January 21, 1976.

†Interview with the Secretary of the Iranian Management Association, November 3, 1975.

Thus the brain drain only compounded the severe manpower shortage in Iran. It is as yet unclear whether many of the Iranians abroad will wish to return under the new political conditions when they stabilize.

Within the private sector itself, the supply of university graduates was further limited because it had to compete with the public service sector, which monopolized a large percentage of the HLM, most of whom had to have university degrees. In 1966, for example, the civil service employed 7 percent of all employed professional, technical, and related personnel and 23 percent of all employed managerial and administrative workers.[36] If one includes those employed in community services, which are primarily government-controlled and -operated, these figures increase to 75 and 35 percent, respectively.[37] These percentages still do not take into account government-owned industry or the military, which generated a large demand for HLM. Also, the fact that the bulk of the government services is located in Tehran only exacerbated the situation, as most private industry and services are also located in Tehran.

Since 1966, significantly higher salaries in the private sector seemed to have caused a greater preference for private sector employment.* However, in December 1975, the government enacted free education legislation. Under the new law Iranian students could obtain free higher-level education provided they served their country in government posts for an equal number of years after they had completed their studies. Of all the students in institutions of higher education in Iran, 95 percent were thought to be part of the free education program in 1976.[38]

The quantity of HLM available to both the public and private sectors, however, is only part of the manpower shortage problem. On the demand side, employers had shown an unwillingness to hire and properly utilize Iranian-educated manpower despite the apparent urgency of their manpower needs. For example, of the approximately 4,000 students who graduated each year from the University of Tehran, "most of them [could] not find jobs."[39]

The difficulties experienced by Iranian-educated graduates were a consequence of the development strategy. The drive to become industrialized in a short period and the attendant emphasis upon capital-intensive projects had necessitated the importation of technology from the advanced nations rather than the slower development of other technological alternatives indigenously. The Iranian educational system has not been able to provide the quality of instruction needed to manage Western technology. In part, quality has been sacrificed by the policies that have attempted to expand enrollment in universities to the point of overloading existing facilities and overutilizing available

---

*This fact is supported by precensus household surveys conducted in 1973–75. The author obtained this information from the directors of the 1976 census at the Statistical Centre of Iran.

teachers.[40] In addition, as is characteristic of educational systems in developing countries, Iran has had to try to reorganize a system of higher education that was originally designed to cater to the needs of the wealthy, arts-oriented civil servant rather than to an industrializing state.

Given these drawbacks of the educational system, foreign-educated manpower, both expatriate and Iranian, seemed to be much better suited to guide the chosen economic strategy. Data shown in Table 2.2, for instance, reveal that foreign-educated Iranians study scientific and technical subjects in much greater proportion than their counterparts in Iranian institutions. Quite apart from the considerations governed by imported technology, the entrepreneurial elite had also shown a social bias for foreign-educated Iranians. As one management consultant put it when interviewed for this study: "The foreign-educated Iranian has much more social finesse and a greater basis for personal appeal to the Iranian employer, who is usually himself a member of the established, well-traveled elite, or fancies himself to be so, than the Iranian who has stayed home."

TABLE 2.2

Field of Study for Iranians Enrolled Abroad and in Iran in Institutions of Higher Education

Field of Study	Iranians Enrolled Abroad* 1974–76		Iranians Enrolled in Iran 1976	
	Number	Percent	Number	Percent
Arts and non-technical subjects	8,499	19.4	76,809	50.6
Scientific and technical subjects	35,422	80.6	75,096	49.4
Total	43,921	100.0	151,905	100.0

Note: This table aggregates categories used in original sources to permit comparison. Arts and non-technical subjects include the study of law, economics and business administration, fine arts, education, agriculture, humanities, and other arts subjects. Scientific and technical subjects include the study of engineering and technology, medicine, mathematics, and the natural sciences.

*Excludes those whose field of study was tallied as "undetermined."

Source: For Iranians enrolled abroad, see "Skills Shortage and the Brain Drain," *Iran Economic Service*, no. 98 (December 1976): 3–4. For Iranians enrolled in Iran, see Institute for Research and Planning in Science and Education, *Statistics of Higher Education in Iran* (Tehran, 1976), p. 34.

CONCLUSIONS

In summary, economic development in Iran was attempted through a process of backward integration. Rather than first developing a strong economic base in the traditional sectors, such as agriculture, or creating necessary infrastructures that would provide stimulus to the modern sector, investment in these areas was reduced by the demands of the industrial sector.[41] These imbalances were widened by the acceleration of industrialization in 1974. After 1974, the high dependence on oil revenues strained to a breaking point the economic expansion efforts—particularly as the oil income was erratic and therefore could not meet the growing demand for support facilities. The result has been hyperinflation and stagnation.

Socially, the development strategy has had very significant consequences. These factors are at the root of many of the tensions that have created the social revolution. The choice of a capital-intensive approach, for instance, has increased the demand for HLM, thereby creating a shortage of such manpower. But the resulting dependence upon imported technology in turn has created very serious malutilization of the human resources educated in Iranian universities. Partly because the Iranian system of higher education has been inconsistent with the demands of Western technology and partly because the entrepreneurs had a bias for Western training, graduates from the national universities, many of whom have struggled to obtain their education in the hopes of social and economic advancement, had been excluded from many opportunities in favor of either Iranians educated abroad or foreigners.

At the more global level, the demand for skilled and high-level manpower has exerted tremendous upward pressure on wage and salary levels for these groups, causing deteriorating economic positions for the urban and rural poor—the unskilled. In addition, the high rates of inflation have reduced real income for the middle and lower classes.[42] Thus the rapid industrialization has been a cause of alienation for these strata of society.

The failure of the industrialization process has been largely a result of the government's inability to create infrastructures or educational systems compatible to the chosen rate and level of economic expansion. The inadequacies of government planning were a product of the sociopolitical environment which is discussed in Chapter 3.

NOTES

1. For a summary of the economic goals set out for the Fifth and Sixth Plans, see *Iran Almanac and Book of Facts, 1976*, 15th ed. (Tehran: Echo of Iran Press, 1976).

2. International Monetary Fund, *International Financial Statistics*, January 1979. In 1976/77, the government deficit was 37.8 billion rials; in 1977/78, it had grown to 414.0 billion rials.

3. See Youssef M. Ibrahim, "Strife Cripples Iran's Economy," *New York Times*, November 28, 1978, for a discussion of the projects that were canceled. Many of these projects were important to the development of Iranian infrastructures, such as highway construction, industrial modernization, and improvement of telecommunications. See also Robert Graham, *Iran: Illusion of Power* (London: St. Mary's Press, 1978), particularly chap. 7.

4. Peter B. Doeringer and Michael J. Piore, *Internal Labor Markets and Manpower Analysis* (Lexington, Mass: Heath, 1971), for example, state that the unique internal organizational policies in the United States were shaped by the course of economic development and pressures exerted by the actors in the marketplace.

5. Robert E. Looney, *A Development Strategy for Iran Through the 1980's* (New York: Praeger, 1977), places five of the oil exporters—Iran, Venezuela, Algeria, Ecuador, and Iraq—in similar categories by virtue of their level of economic development and position to make the most effective use of the increase in oil revenues granted them by the 1973 increase in oil prices.

6. Jahangir Amuzegar and M. Ali Fekrat, *Iran: Economic Development Under Dualistic Conditions* (Chicago: University of Chicago Press, 1971), p. 127.

7. See Iranian Plan and Budget Organization, Planometrics Bureau, *Iran's Fifth Development Plan 1973-1978: Revised—A Summary* (Tehran; 1974). It should be pointed out that the actual level of money invested in the agricultural sector was not so much a problem as was the lack of administrative priority given to the sector.

8. Ann Lambton, *The Persian Land Reform 1962-1966* (London: Oxford University Press, 1969); and Oddvar Aresvik, *The Agricultural Development of Iran* (New York: Praeger, 1976), discuss development in the agricultural sector.

9. See Looney, op. cit., p. 76. This figure is below the official government figures but has been considered more accurate by agricultural experts.

10. Graham, op. cit., p. 43.

11. *New York Times*, November 28, 1978, p. D6.

12. W. W. Rostow, *The Stages of Economic Growth* (Cambridge: Cambridge University Press, 1960), emphasizes the importance of the agricultural sector in the development process.

13. See Graham, op. cit., for discussions of the relationship between fluctuations in oil revenues and economic performance.

14. Ibid, p. 38.

15. For history of the growth of the industrial sector, see Julian Bharier, *Economic Development in Iran: 1900-1970* (London: Oxford University Press, 1971).

16. See Reza Razmara, "Employment in Iranian Industry," in *Employment and Unemployment Problems in the Near East and South Asia*, ed. Ronald G. Ridker and Harold Lubell, vol. 3 (New Dehli: Vikas Publications, 1971), p. 659. The oil industry is excluded from these figures.

17. Information was obtained from officials at the Manpower Statistics Department, Ministry of Labor and Social Affairs, Tehran. See also Fred Halliday, *Iran: Dictatorship and Development* (London: Penguin, 1979), p. 182.

18. R. Mabro, "Industry," working paper no. 5, prepared for *Employment and Incomes Policies in Iran* (Geneva: International Labor Organization, 1973), considers these estimates to be the best.

19. Bank Markazi Iran, Economic Statistics Department, Industrial Statistics Section, *Survey of the Selected Manufacturing Industries in 1353* (1974/75) (Tehran, 1975). Note: Years are numbered differently in Iran and the calendar year is from March 21 to March 20. In the Persian calendar, March 21, 1974 to March 20, 1975 was 1353.

20. Graham, op. cit., p. 120. Graham cites as his source the U. S. Embassy, *Semi-Annual Economic Trends Report* (Tehran, May 1977).

21. Ministry of Economy, *1968 Industrial Statistics* (Tehran, 1968).

22. Bank Markazi Iran, op. cit. Official statistics for the latter part of the 1970s are more difficult to obtain. But overall employment has suffered, as has output. For example, the *New York Times*, November 28, 1978, D1, reports that at least 60,000 factory workers had been laid off.

23. For example, Statistical Centre of Iran, *National Census of Population and Housing* for 1956 and 1966, states that professional, technical, and related personnel and administrative and managerial personnel comprise 1.6 and 2.9 percent of the total employed population in these respective years. But, because of the broad definition given to industry, the percentages of the same persons in industrial employment alone are too insignificant to allow for adequate analysis.

24. See Amuzegar and Fekrat, op. cit., p. 65. This trend continued into the 1970s. See Fereidun Fesharaki, *The Development of Iranian Oil Industry* (London: Praeger, 1976).

25. G. Psacharopoulos and G. Williams, "Education and Vocational Training," working paper no. 8, prepared for *Employment and Incomes Policies in Iran* (Geneva: International Labor Organization, 1973), discuss these figures.

26. See M. H. Pesaran, "Income Distribution and Its Major Determinants in Iran," in *Iran: Past, Present and Future: The Persepolis Symposium*, ed. Jan Jacqz (New York: Aspen Institute for Humanistic Studies, 1976), pp. 267–86.

27. "Employment of Foreign Nationals in Iran," *Iran Economic Service*, no. 64 (December 30, 1975): 11.

28. Hamideh Asadi, "Some Reflections on the Problems of Importing Skilled Manpower," (Tehran: Plan and Budget Organization, 1975), mimeographed, p. 4, sets this figure at 20,581 in 1975.

29. *The Times*, London, England, May 22, 1975.

30. Asadi, op. cit., pp. 4–5.

31. "Employment of Foreign Nationals in Iran," op. cit., p. 11. Despite this attitude, the government employed 26 percent of all foreigners in Iran excluding those working under the auspices of international organizations, such as the International Labor Organization, the World Bank, and the United Nations.

32. "Manpower Deficit in Iran," *Iran Economic Service*, no. 35 (June 3, 1975): 10.

33. *Iran Almanac and Book of Facts, 1976*, op. cit., p. 344.

34. "Skills Shortage and the Brain Drain," *Iran Economic Service*, no. 98 (December 14, 1976): 3–4. There is a large discrepancy in the statistics because many of the students abroad have other than Iranian student passports.

35. Marvin Zonis, *The Political Elite of Iran* (Princeton, N.J.: Princeton University Press, 1971), p. 52. See also George B. Baldwin, "Four Studies on the Iranian Brain Drain," in *The International Migration of High-Level Manpower* (New York: Praeger, 1970), pp. 374–96.

36. Statistical Centre of Iran, *National Census of Population and Housing, 1966.*

37. Ibid.

38. "Education Is the Largest Industry in Iran—Sami'i," *Kayhan International*, September 5, 1976, p. 3.

39. "Shortages of Skills Due to Bad Planning," *Kayhan International*, August 19, 1976, p. 8.

40. *New York Times*, November 18, 1978, relates, for example, that university enrollments have doubled in seven years.

41. Albert O. Hirschman, *The Strategy of Economic Development* (New Haven, Conn.: Yale University Press, 1961), perceives that this is not an unwise course of development. But he did not envision the rapidity of growth in induced demand.

42. Inflation figures published by the government are misleading because they have been doctored and do not take into account black market costs or the relative importance

of certain items, such as the cost of land (see Graham, op. cit., p. 91). However, inflation generally has been acknowledged to be between 30 and 40 percent during 1974-75. Wages during the period have also increased a similar amount (see International Monetary Fund, op. cit.). But the wage gains have been substantially reaped more by some groups in the labor market than by others.

3

THE SOCIO–POLITICAL ENVIRONMENT OF IRAN

In theory, Iran has been a constitutional monarchy since 1906. Under the Shah, there was a parliament comprised of a lower house (the Majles) of 268 seats and a 60-seat Senate and, until 1975, a multiparty system. But these had been only trappings for a democracy that, in fact, did not exist. The center of power rested until 1979 with the Shah, who had not been above tampering with election results.[1]

That the royal personage, or indeed a strong personality with either religious or military authority, along with an established elite, should wield such power has historical foundation in Iran:

> From the earliest days of Iranian greatness . . . , there has been a highly articulated social structure whose divisions were always well defined and recognized. Moreover, an explicitly identified elite group has existed for the same period, an elite group which was differentially rewarded as, it was assumed, was their rightful dessert.[2]

In this light, the present political struggles in Iran may be viewed as an effort to articulate and establish a new elite and social order that is different but not radically divergent from historical experiences.

Wealth, and to some extent proven competence, have always been considered more important for elite membership than one's position at birth. This elite social structure therefore embodies what Marvin Zonis calls "the ideology of an open class system."[3] The rise to power by the present Shah's father, who began his life as a peasant, is partly explained by this ideology. However, the actual degree of social mobility has been very limited. The vast majority of Iranians do not possess the wealth to qualify for elite membership or the means with which to achieve it, such as access to formal education, high-level personal connections, military strength, or the ability to marry well.

Nevertheless, the open class ideology had been most useful in justifying the Shah's maneuvers to raise some persons to high social positions and to lower the positions of others, and for removing a prime cause for social conflict on class terms until the beginnings of civil dissent in 1978 that was to be his downfall. In fact, this dissent is largely founded in the realization that the open class ideology was not operative, that is, the less advantaged did not see mobility as a strong possibility, particularly in light of the economic stagnation caused by the failures of rapid industrialization and the favoritism shown by it to the educated and skilled minority.

But it would be foolhardy to attribute to history alone the foundations of the Shah's personal power, which extended beyond that of any elite group. Many features of the Shah's particular administrative style have been responsible for his present position. They are described below.

GEOGRAPHICAL CENTRALIZATION OF POWER

According to the Fifth Plan, the Ministry of the Interior was to make "an attempt . . . to confine the ministries in Tehran to staff work . . . and to transfer executive functions to provincial offices and departments."[4] However, Tehran is still the focal point of political, social, and economic life in Iran. Of the 19 ostans (provinces) and 3 farmandari-kols (territories) in Iran, none has its own parliaments or constiutions. Governors were appointed by officials from Tehran with the approval of the Shah, and municipalities relied upon the central government for most of their revenues.

Tehran, which encompasses 14 percent of Iran's population, also has reaped a disproportionate amount of the advantages of development. Tehran accounts for 51 percent of Iran's production of manufactured goods, 30 percent of the industrial enterprises, 60 percent of all wages and salaries, 33 percent of total investment, 35 percent of the country's gross national product, 38 percent of all institutions of higher education, 52 percent of all students in higher education, 46 percent of all doctors, 76 percent of all cars, and 100 percent of all banks, insurance companies, and other fiduciary institutions, all of which have their headquarters in Tehran.[5]

Thus, anyone who wished to be active within Tehran society had to maintain contact with Tehran, and to be politically powerful had to live there.[6] Businessmen from Esphahan who provided background information for this study felt that they were incapable of influencing events in Iran because they did not live in Tehran. In order to carry on their personal everyday affairs, in fact, it was necessary for them to make frequent trips to Tehran for consultations with bankers, government officials, and technical advisers.

Centralization of power is a necessary political expedient in Iran where there are diverse cultural groups who historically have posed significant threats to the national power. However, centralization has been responsible for the conflict-creating economic disparities between Tehran and most urban and particularly the rural areas.

CONTROL OVER THE BUREAUCRACY, THE LEGISLATURE, AND THE MILITARY

The Shah had great power over the administrative and military bodies of his realm by virtue of his constitutional authority to appoint the persons who were to occupy the most influential positions. As commander-in-chief of the armed forces, he conferred military ranks and was entitled to declare war and conclude peace. Apart from being able to call special sessions of parliament or to dissolve it, he appointed 30 of the 60 persons of the Senate. He also selected the prime minister and approved the selection of the cabinet ministers, the governor of the Central Bank, and the head of the National Iranian Oil Company (NIOC), all of whom headed the staffs of his government service. His power to discharge these persons helped to ensure that they carried out his wishes. Moreover, although efforts were made to appoint cabinet ministers who could work together, the same did not hold true for other positions. Frequently, personal enemies would head different institutions.[7] Such a phenomenon naturally prevented a meaningful working relationship among these various groups.

To ensure the diversification of control, the Shah divided responsibility for important matters of the state among the various agencies so that no single person or agency could monopolize some information or perform some duty that made him indispensable to the system. There are many illustrations of this behavior. To mention one, the Council for the Expansion of Public Ownership of Productive Units was in charge of overseeing the execution of the share participation laws (to be discussed below) included the ministers of seven departments, the governor the the Central Bank, and the president of the Chamber of Commerce, Industries and Mines.

But perhaps the most essential technique of the Shah's form of administration, from the point of view of political control of the elite, was the prevalence of his participation in the actual decision-making process. By holding regular and private audiences with the individual officials of his various committees, he gained information on the issues from all involved individuals separately. He also was present at as many cabinet meetings as possible, and therefore was the leading decision maker in these cases.[8]

This form of the Shah's style of rule, while it was seemingly effective in the short run in controlling political opposition, was the major cause behind the bungling of the Fifth Plan. At the time of the revision of the plan immediately after the oil price increases in 1974, the Shah was so intent upon accelerating the industrialization process, while at the same time soliciting favor from diverse social groups with greatly expanded welfare measures, that any opposition to the grandiose schemes was squelched.[9]

Administrative style also had a pertinent impact upon the internal operation of the civil service. Most individuals in charge of government organizations and committees, out of fear of incurring the Shah's displeasure and the desire for self-aggrandizement, would neither make decisions independently of the Shah nor delegate authority. The result was a very ineffective and inefficient bureaucracy, which made policy implementation and particularly the detailed design and coordination of efforts necessary to overcome the drawbacks to the intent implied by the Fifth Plan, impossible.[10] The operation of the day-to-day affairs of the government, in fact, accounted for an overrun of 18 percent on average over budget.[11]

The inability of the government service to impose effective limits upon the planning process meant that the Fifth Plan became more a design for political control than economic expansion with implied retarding effects upon economic growth. Resources were directed toward too diverse a range of activities from investments abroad, to steel mills, to textile plants, and to a variety of welfare measures. This diversity detracted from essential investment in infrastructures and education. In the final analysis, government policy either antagonized or substituted for rather than complemented private initiatives in modern sector. By the time Iamshed Amouzegar became prime minister in August 1977 and attempted to bring the economy under control, high expectations had already been developed and the willingness to accept economic restraint under the Shah was not forthcoming. His attempt to use the Iranian revenues as the "carrot and the stick" to curry political support had ironically backfired.

POLITICAL CONTROL

The Shah, in *Mission for My Country* (1974), stated:

If I were a dictator rather than a constitutional monarch, then I might be tempted to sponsor a single dominant party such as Hitler organized or such as you find today in Communist countries. But, as a constitutional monarch, I can afford to encourage large-scale party activity free from the strait jacket of one-party rule or the one-party state.[12]

On March 1, 1975, he made an about-face and announced that:

Today we lay the foundation of a new political structure—the Resurrection of Iran. . . . Every Iranian who has clarified his position, that

is, who believes in the Constitution, the Monarchy and the Sixth
Bahman Revolution, must definitely join this political organization.
All will be equal; all will have a single structure. Within this great
structure, differences in taste will be authorized on the basis of these
three principles.[13]

Thus the Resurrection, or Rastakhiz, party came into being. It was further
announced that "those who did not believe in the three principles could live
freely in Iran 'obviously without expecting to have a say in running national
affairs.' Those who [actively] opposed these principles [could be] given safe
conduct to leave the country."[14] Only members of the armed forces were
exempted from having to join the party and could, at the same time, maintain
high positions. Keeping the military separate from these affairs was, it seemed, a
politically wise move not inconsistent with the rest of the Shah's form of rule.

The reactions to this announcement were immediate. By May 1975,
only two months later, Iran's four existing political parties, the Iranian Student
Organization, the majority of the 4,500 delegates of the Congress of Workers,
and various organizations in Tehran and the provinces had announced their
membership in the Rastakhiz party. By the end of the year, new elections under
the one-party system had been held, and an extensive political organization had
been set up to handle internal administration, finances, and discipline and to
oversee the many study committees that were formed to consider all matters
affecting the nation and its development.

Considering the reactions to this call for unification under one party,
it is not too difficult to see how effective a control device the party was in-
tended to be to the Shah. By insisting upon membership in a party with majority
support, the Shah excluded from power all those outside its confines. By further
stressing that those who were "good" and "true" party members (the only kind
allowable) showed their loyalty by actively supporting the principles devised for
the party, he curbed any forceful official opposition by expelling from the party
any dissenting individual.* Also, because the persons who headed the party
bureaucracy and its committees were the same people who staffed the civil
service, the party justified the administration's involvement in all aspects of
Iranian life.

For the effect one-party rule had upon removing opposition from the
realm of acceptable behavior, one can refer to the annual summary of events of
the first parliament under the one-party system. It reads:

---

*The party was nominally divided into two wings—the progressive versus the con-
structive liberals, for the purposes of channeling debate, although it was not obligatory to
belong to either side. These divisions were essentially meaningless. All final decisions were
made by the Central Council and Executive Committee.

> There [was] no majority or minority as such (in the Parliament).
> . . . For this reason, all bills [were] approved almost unanimously.
> Those who took part in the debate had not registered to speak in the
> debate as "against" it and in their speeches therefore they just made
> certain statements. For the first time, the list of speakers had not
> been drawn in two sections—"for" and "against."[15]

All private industrial establishments researched for this study also mentioned the party's involvements with the workers in their plants. One manager, for instance, complained that the establishment had lost three days' production in two months because the party had come to hold rallies with the workers.

In the autumn of 1978, the Shah attempted to placate growing political opposition by rescinding the one-party rule. As the usefulness of the party to central opposition was by that time clearly terminated, the Shah's action merely revealed his weakness and could not be viewed as a sincere gesture toward liberalization. By removing official opposition with the institution of the party, he had earlier provided an outlet for growing "unofficial" dissent, the momentum of which could not be stopped.

Adjuncts to the political party were the intelligence organizations set up to gather "politically sensitive information." These were the Sazman-e-Ettala'at va Amniyate Keshvar (State Security and Intelligence Organization, commonly known as SAVAK); the Special Intelligence Bureau, which was a physically and a financially independent branch of SAVAK; and the J-2 branch of the Imperial Armed Forces. SAVAK was in charge of general intelligence, while the latter two organizations, in accordance with the Shah's penchant for overlapping responsibilities, were charged with duplicating SAVAK's work in matters considered to pose a serious threat to national stability.[16]

It had been rumored that about one in eleven of all Iranian were SAVAK informants.[17] Iranian employees within every organization, for example, took a "delight" in informing the initiate about who was officially SAVAK and who was suspected of being connected. Whatever validity there was to these rumors, the fact remained that the belief in this wide-scale observance, while not discouraging personal comments, prohibited public expression of discontent by all except the most committed.

PRIVATE SECTOR CONTROL THROUGH OWNERSHIP

The Shah and his family were able to gain a measure of control over the private industrial establishments through direct ownership. Every large establishment in Iran needed the Shah's blessing to remain operative. As a result, industrialists generally gave the Shah shares in the operation. (One businessman who was interviewed for this study stated that 10 percent was customary.) These shares were never in the Shah's name, and rarely in those of his family, but in the name of one of the organizations he controlled. The most commonly mentioned organizations in this regard were the Pahlavi Foundation and Bank Omran.[18] Shares in the enterprises were usually too small to involve the holding organizations directly with the day-to-day administration of the company but were large enough to give the royal family access to confidential information and to allow audits conducted by their own personnel.

LEGAL POLICIES

Apart from ownership, the Shah's government policed the private sector through a series of laws. As mentioned earlier, the government bureaucracies in Iran did not possess the efficiency with which to apply the law properly. The laws were also written in such a way as to be at times incomprehensible and at other times contradictory. Moreover, under the Shah, they were often amended with such rapidity, and without prior notification, that it was difficult to be knowledgeable of the changes. As such, the means of control offered by these statutes did not lie with the administration's ability to apply the law equally and in an unbiased fashion to everyone. The laws were powerful because their very existence permitted the government to reward and punish selectively.[19]

The pertinent laws are licensing, import-export, antiprofiteering, share participation, and labor legislation.

Licensing

Licensing in Iran, which was first conceived in the 1950s, was a system designed to control ostensibly the structure of industrial development by offering incentives and protection to investors, Iranian and foreign, who, through a formal application and evaluation process, proved themselves to have the best managerial, technical, and financial capabilities to implement a desired project. Licensing was not originally a legal requirement. But those firms that did not have a license were at a disadvantage. Only licensed investors enjoyed import tariff exemptions for capital and intermediate goods, protection from foreign competitors in the form of tariff barriers, tax holidays, eligibility for low interest loans and industrial rates for electrical power and water, options to buy government land at nominal prices, easy access to municipal building permits, export incentives, and an implied commitment of government support in the event of economic difficulties.[20]

In principle, licensing laws represent sound policy for a developing nation that would like to have some say in how capital resources are utilized, how much foreign investment is permitted, and to have the size, number, location, and products of enterprises in any one industry controlled. They also can encourage entrepreneurship, which is generally in short supply. In practice, however, the licensing laws in Iran could not achieve these goals. From the legal point of view, the laws specified a confusing array of elaborate regulations necessary for the application of a license, but did not clearly define how one proposal would be judged better than another. Furthermore, there was neither a consistent long-run plan from which administrators could work nor the experts capable of assessing the relative merits of the proposals.

As a result, the licensing laws have been criticized for being discriminatory against the small investor who did not have the resources to qualify for a license and against some large investors who have complained that their applications were ignored rather than processed fairly. In effect, the licensing laws have, by limiting the expansion of the entrepreneurial class, ensured that industry was controlled by a small handful of favored elite. On the negative side, the removal of government support as granted under licensing helped to see that these businessmen did not overtly defy the government. On the positive side, the laws ensured entrepreneurs substantial rewards from their investments. Many of the Iranian entrepreneurs were not only willing to give the Shah a financial return from their operations but were also directly or indirectly through an immediate family member active participants in the Shah's government.

The small size of the entrepreneurial class and the protection given to its endeavours by virtue of political connections have meant that good management practices have not been encouraged and consequently efficient technological choices that would have better utilized Iran's educated manpower were not explored.[21] In the final analysis, of course, the fall of the Shah's regime has also meant the flight of the most committed of the leading entrepreneurs from Iran who transferred large sums of money out of the country in 1978 in anticipation of the political turmoil.

Import-Export Laws

These laws were essential counterparts to the licensing system, as they accounted for many of the incentives offered by the above policy. They also allowed the government to limit exports when domestic production was needed for internal consumption and to pass into the country consumer and intermediate goods at favorable tariff rates when it was felt that the local manufacturers of these goods needed incentives to improve their efficiency.*

But changes in the import-export regulations were often motivated by

---

*For this reason import tariffs on sugar and, in 1976, household appliances had been reduced. Similarly, many industries during the boom were not allowd to export their products because their output was needed for domestic consumption. Due to Iran's poor comparative advantage for consumer durables, exports have never figured prominently in the modern sector.

short-run personal and political gain rather than by the national interest.* In situations where they have been used properly as a complement to licensing regulations, they were known to be so cavalierly controlled that their purpose was negated.† The laws, moreover, were subject to so many frequent changes that one businessman interviewed for the study commented that: "I need at least one individual on the job at all times who does nothing but try to establish what the law is." Thus, rather than providing a stabilizing influence, they became another means for preferential reward and punishment and a source of royal corruption.

Antiprofiteering Regulations

The control of prices has had a long history. But its effect upon the private sector had not been strongly felt until 1975. Prior to 1973, there was a Department of Price Review in the now defunct Ministry of Economy that monitored the prices of goods and services purchased by government departments. In October 1973, the Shah, alarmed over rising prices, established the Price Commission (PC) as an independent body of the Ministry of Commerce. The commission's job was to review and advise on how prices should be fixed with the stipulation

---

*For example, in 1975–76, the import tariffs on English Land-Rovers was reduced considerably so that anyone could bring in a Land-Rover for the cost of the vehicle plus 4 percent. In September 1976, however, the tariff was again raised so that a Land-Rover cost the basic selling price, transportation costs to Iran, and 200 percent tax. The rumor circulating at the time was that the import duties were again imposed because the Shah's brother had brought so many Land-Rovers into the country at the low cost that he wanted to sell them at a very high profit. A businessman interviewed for this study also claimed that tariff restrictions on products from foreign competitors were unfairly being lifted on the basis of promoting industry efficiency. Many other industries were not being so treated.

†For example, the Iranian Ball-Bearing Company was licensed with the guarantee from the government that the importation of ball bearings from other countries would be illegal. Despite this ban on competitors' products, however, the company found itself in severe financial difficulties. A case writer from the Iran Centre for Management Studies set out to study the situation, which seemed difficult to understand because the company had a virtual monopoly in the industry and was partly owned by one of its major customers, Iran National, the largest automotive firm in Iran. The case writer found that the company's ball bearings were not selling because the automotive firms, including Iran National, were all importing ball bearings illegally through the ports in the south of Iran!

that, unless justified cause was shown, prices were to be rolled back to the June 1973 level. Because of the limited staff accorded to the PC, the policy had little impact. From March 1974 to July 1975, increases in wages and the cost of raw materials were passed on to the consumer.

On August 6, 1975, however, the Shah firmly established a campaign against profiteering and hoarding by establishing these measures as the four-teenth principle of the Sixth Bahman Revolution (the name given to the Shah's reform movement). Concurrent with this announcement, a Rastakhiz party com-mittee (composed mostly of students), the National Commission for Consumer Protection, and the Guild Chambers (which have the power to fine, close down, or send to court offending shopkeepers) established themselves as the watchdogs for the PC whose job was to investigate cases of infractions that these bodies forwarded to it. Guilty parties could be tried by a military tribunal set up for the occasion; this resulted in the imprisonment or deportation of many. Since Nov-ember 1975, the PC investigated reasons for the shortages of goods or price in-creases when reported by government authorities, and recommended prices at the request of industrial concerns that sought price increases due to rising costs.

The administration of the antiprofiteering laws between August and November 1975 is one of the most blatant examples of the biased administra-tion of the law. During this period some prominent businessmen were indeed arrested. However, the number actually arrested relative to the number of known violaters of the law was minimal. The application of the law in these instances served a dual purpose. First, it served to underscore what could be the possible consequences should businessmen not make a show of following the guidelines of the Shah's reform movement and, second, it was a political move attempting to show to the average consumer that government policy was serious-ly directed toward safeguarding real income. In point of fact, the laws were impossible to follow exactly because there were no guidelines establishing what a fair profit was.*

---

*It was generally believed that profit margins were to be set at 10 to 15 percent above cost. However, this figure had no foundation in the law, and was only the product of misinformed press reports. In general, the antiprofiteering law had been used to attack persons selling everyday consumer items, such as food, meals in restaurants, and flowers. Prices on items that were not significant components of daily consumption were not effec-tively controlled. The auto industry, in fact, was granted an explicit exemption from the price laws. Nonetheless, the very inflated black market prices of automobiles were well known. Persons buying cars through regular channels, indeed, had to wait months for their purchase because the black market buyers had first priority. (Source of information on the PC and its policies was obtained from a highly placed official in the PC.)

Share Participation Law

In May 1972, the Shah launched the general scheme for share participation. The guidelines stated that 99 percent of the shares of state-owned production units, excluding key industries, and 49 percent of the shares of private mining and production units must be sold to workers, farmers, and eventually the general public by October 1978. In the case of the government industries, 1 percent ownership accounted for managerial control. Eligible companies had to have at least a registered capital of 100 million rials ($1.5 million), fixed assets of 200 million rials ($3 million), or a minimum turnover of 250 million rials per year ($3.75 million) and a record of production of five years or more. The first batch of eligible companies made their first share offers by March 22, 1976.

The law also set up various bodies to supervise its enactment, and to buy the shares for transfer to the workers and farmers as their first priority. Under the law, foreign ownership in joint ventures was limited to 15 to 30 percent, depending upon the industry. The maximum amount of money that a worker, farmer, or private investor could spend on a new share issue was also stipulated.[22]

While superficially designed to enhance the Shah's position with the general public, the plan, like land reform, excluded large numbers of persons, particularly the majority of workers who were employed in small establishments. But the possible control implications of the share participation law were obvious. By taking 49 percent of the company shares away from the large industrial owner, the power of an industrialist could be severely curtailed. In that 49 percent of the shares would be divided among small investors, or kept in trust by the government, the Shah's power to manipulate this block of shares (should it become necessary) was considerable. Moreover, the block of shares that the Shah and his family owned in most large industrial enterprises could become relatively more significant if the percentage of shares owned by the other major shareholders was reduced.*

Since the time of its inception, the share participation law caused considerable anxiety among businessmen. In point of fact, the law was used as selectively as were the others. By July 1977, only 151 of the original 320 companies scheduled to participate in the plan had actually done so, and of them, only 20 percent of their scheduled shares had been distributed.[23] The other

---

*Many, in fact, did not expect that the Shah would give up any of the percentage of the shares he or his family owned through the auspices of the holding organization in any one company when the shares were redistributed to the public. If such was the case, the Shah's share would be relatively large compared to that of the other investors.

companies were able to negotiate an indefinite postponement to their involvement in the plan, largely because businessmen in Iran, particularly foreign, made curtailment of the share participation scheme the condition for their continued investment.

However, the Shah's attempt to affect private ownership while seemingly to cater to the interests of disgruntled workers and farmers in conjunction with his antiprofiteering campaign and arbitrary export-import laws had a harmful impact upon business confidence. Entrepreneurs realized that the Shah was quite willing to use them to satisfy his own political needs. The exodus of capital out of the country, which became most notable in 1978, actually had begun before that time. With the exception of one, businessmen who were interviewed for this study in 1976 all stated that they were slowly turning fixed assets into cash to send abroad. Others also mentioned that they expected they would leave the country in a few years time. In light of these actions, the lack of active support the Shah received from the entrepreneurial class during 1978 and 1979 seems more comprehensible.

Labor Legislation

The labor legislation that covers all employees being paid a wage or salary in private establishments of more than ten employees was first conceived in 1959 and amended at later periods. The law granted the right to form trade unions, professional organizations, or employer associations providing approval and supervision is accepted from the Ministry of Labor and Social Affairs, and gave the right to bargain collectively provided any unresolved dispute was placed before a tripartite Dispute Settlement Board for final and binding arbitration.[24]

The law accorded to the employee certain other rights and benefits with which the employer must comply. For instance, under the law the employee was given protection against unfair dismissals through appeals to the Dispute Settlement Board. Should a dismissal be ruled as unfair the employer was obliged to pay damages. The law also made mandatory provision for social security benefits (which were extended to staff employees only in 1971) and for participation in profit-sharing schemes that yielded the employees an annual bonus of one to three months' salary depending on the industry. This was distinct from the share participation plan described previously.

The government could also stipulate minimum wages, supervise wage and salary increases, demand a job evaluation plan for all factories employing over 100 employees, and close down private employment agencies in favor of those operated by the government. Under the law, regulations governing the employment of foreign nationals were defined as well.

The administration of the labor laws has been criticized as being very biased toward labor.[25] This bias often resulted in contradictory policies. For instance, the announcement of the new minimum wage regulations in March 1976 stipulated that all wages in the industrial sector should increase by a set formula, amounting to an across-the-board settlement. Simultaneously, the Ministry of Labor stated that employers, according to the new pricing policies, were obliged to keep wages down. When one employer in this study pointed out that he could not possibly grant an across-the-board settlement and curb wages, he was told to grant an across-the-board increase to keep his workers happy, but that he was not to mention that he was officially told to do so.

Out of all the groups in the industrial labor market, production labor is the weakest because it is the poorest and least educated of all groups. For this reason, the production workers are the most susceptible to becoming puppets of some other interest group, either the government or the employer. The labor legislation and the way in which it was administered ensured that it was the government that co-opted this group.

By not permitting trade union organization without government consent and involvement, the government was able essentially to manage trade union activity by allying its leadership with the party and official government reform movement.[26] Any trade union protest was thereby directed away from government targets toward the employer. In return for their loyalty and their attendance at party rallies, the workers were rewarded with labor legislation in their favor. HLM, specifically, being unorganized despite the provisions for professional organizations, maintained no central voice except insofar as they were allied with the general principles of the employed (rather than the employer).

The end result of the various legal control measures was that the government and state institutions held the balance of power among the participants in the labor market. Moreover, in light of the fact that the civil service was personally controlled by the Shah, the final authority in the marketplace rested with him.

More specifically, the Shah was able to preserve his balance of power because of his ability to seduce or threaten persons into joining his cause, on the one hand, and his agility at keeping protagonists divided from one another, on the other hand. To take one example, the industrialists were rewarded for their loyalty by the favorable provisions of the licensing laws, and the implicit understanding that they would be permitted to continue making high profits, provided they did not openly oppose or deviate form the official government position. Should they stray from the stated policy, however, licenses could be revoked, import-export laws changed, profiteering charges leveled, and a variety of more subtle sanctions applied—in rapid succession.

The Shah was able to oversee industrialists' actions through his direct ownership in the firms, the centralization of power, particularly financial power, in Tehran, and through the ever-watchful eyes of SAVAK and the party, the latter which was permitted into firms through the trade unions. The constant observation ensured that employers   would not unite against the government. Similarly, the government involvement guaranteed that workers did not coalesce with or be overly patronized by the employer. In this light, the share partici- pation law was particularly effective in giving more control to the government.

What the Shah did not seem to realize was that this system of control could work only so long as employees perceived that industrialization would accord them with increasing real incomes and heightened social status, and the entrepreneurs were making profits high enough to compensate them for their risk in an uncertain environment. In the aftermath of the economic boom that ended in 1976, profit levels declined and the overriding political intent of legislation that was thinly disguised under the banner of social reform became a source of strong opposition to the Shah.

CONCLUSIONS

The failures of economic development outlined in Chapter 2 can be related to the limitations of government planning in Iran. The inability to voice opposi- tion to the grandiose goals formulated by the Shah in 1974, compounded by bureaucracy made inefficient by self-interested elitist control and lack of experience, prevented the development of explicit blueprints for economic ex- pansion and led to a diversification of government resources away from measures that in the long-run could have either satisfied the high expectations developed in the general populace or complemented private initiatives to become a modern state. The direction imposed upon the planning process by the Shah, and second- arily by his appointed elite, was ultimately a destabilizing effect of the sociopoli- tical system.

The spirit of the Shah's policies as judged by the selective way in which they were applied for reward and punishment as was deemed politically ex- pedient showed the Shah as unwilling to liberalize his society despite his rhetoric. Ultimately, his downfall was in his attempt to graft industrial revolution to a traditional social structure designed to maintain his personal power.

The government policies had a significant impact upon the choice of technology in the private sector. On the one hand, the artificially high wage rates and associated labor costs instituted by labor legislation and the ingress of the party and SAVAK into the firms through workers' congresses were deterents to the labor-intensive approach. On the other hand, the virtual monopolies and favorable financial discounts offered to private entrepreneurs under the licensing laws made the capital-intensive approach feasible.[27] This is particularly so in light of the fact that lecenses were only granted those who were able to put forward high-cost projects, which made them the most politically prestigious. Economic feasibility, particularly with respect to comparative advantage was of lesser concern as projects could not be properly evaluated. The result was a bias toward industrial establishments making large capital outlays for technology imported from the West. These were also preferred by the entrepreneurial class, who were neither encouraged to nor in general capable at the outset of industrial expansion of exploring other technological alternatives. As mentioned earlier, this approach limited the use of Iran's human resources, particularly the Iranian-educated.

The control aspects of the Shah's policies not only succeeded in finally alienating many diverse groups in the society but also had an impact upon organizational behavior from the outset of industrial expansion. In short, the sociopolitical situation delayed the transition from elitist-based organizations common to traditional societies in both the public and the private sector. The restriction of organizational responsibility to a few carried with it important consequences for HLM. The following section offers an analysis of organizational processes as they relate to this group.

NOTES

1. The most notable incident of election tampering was in 1960 under Prime Minister Eqbal. Eqbal had to give up his position as prime minister as a result of the public outrage following the discovery of his illegal activities on behalf of the Shah. He spent some time in posts abroad and later returned to take over as chairman of the National Iranian Oil Company before his death. See Marvin Zonis, *The Political Elite of Iran* (Princeton, N. J.: Princeton University Press, 1976), pp. 61-63.

2. Ibid., p. 122. For an analysis of social structure in Iran, see also James A. Bill, *The Politics of Iran: Groups, Classes and Modernization* (Columbus, Ohio: Merrill, 1972).

3. Zonis, op. cit.

4. *Iran Almanac: 1966*, 5th ed. (Tehran: Echo of Iran Press, 1966), p. 103.

5. Sources for these statistics are *Iran Almanac: 1966* and *1976*; and Institute for Research and Planning in Science and Education, *Statistics of Higher Education in Iran* (Tehran, 1976).

6. Zonis, op. cit., found that all but five of the respondents in his sample of political elite lived in Tehran.

7. See *ibid*., p. 83, for some examples.

8. Leonard Binder, *Iran: Political Development in a Changing Society* (Berkeley: University of California Press, 1962), p. 118, states that the Shah met with his cabinet once in every three meetings. Zonis, op. cit., p. 95, says it was more frequent.

9. See Robert Graham, *Iran: The Illusion of Power* (London: St. Mary's Press, 1978), for an informative discussion of what went on behind the scenes when the Fifth Plan was revised, particularly chap. 5.

10. George B. Baldwin, *Planning and Development in Iran* (Baltimore: Johns Hopkins Press, 1967), attributes the failure of development planning in Iran chiefly to the ineffiency of the bureaucracy.

11. Graham, op. cit., p. 85.

12. Mohammed Reza Shah Pahlavi, *Mission for My Country* (London: Hutchinson, 1974), p. 173. The first edition of this book came out in 1961.

13. *Iran Almanac: 1976*, p. 107.

14. Ibid., p. 108.
15. Ibid., p. 91.
16. For a discussion of the intelligence organizations, see Zonis, op. cit., pp. 85-87. Graham, op. cit., pp. 140-42, also describes the role the Imperial Inspectorate had in investigating economic, social, and political affairs independently of the other intelligence agencies, especially with reference to the civil service and government-related organizations.
17. Eric Rouleau, "Iran: The Myth and the Reality: Part I," the *Guardian*, October 24, 1976, p. 12, states: "Diplomatic circles put the strength of this ubiquitious force [SAVAK] at 50,000 full-time professional employees and three million part-time informers who keep their eyes and ears open in public establishments, government departments, schools, factories, and fashionable gatherings." Iran has a population of around 33 million, which means one in eleven was a SAVAK informer according to these statistics.
18. The Bank Omran is, in fact, wholly owned by the Pahlavi Foundation. The foundation was supposed to be a charitable organization but its charitable works are reputed to be a minimal part of its budget. For a discussion of these organizations see Graham, op. cit., pp. 155-65 and appendix, pp. 214-17, which outlines the foundation's known assets in December 1977. This list is comprehensive but not entirely complete. Firms researched for this study, for example, reported involvement by the foundation or Bank Omran but were not included on this list.
19. Zonis, op. cit., has suggested that the Shah purposely encouraged infractions of the law so that he could have a case against everyone or anyone should he need it at a later date.
20. One of the best discussions on licensing in Iran is contained in Olga Richardson's, "Industrial Licensing" (Tehran: Iran Centre for Management Studies, 1976), mimeographed. Working papers were available from the centre. Its status, at the time of this writing, is unknown however. A copy may be obtained from the author.
21. Lawrence J. White, "The Evidence on Appropriate Factor Proportions for Manufacturing in Less Developed Countries: A Survey," *Economic Development and Cultural Change*, October 1978, relates how good management and the ability to perceive labor-capital substitution possibilities have been found to be inevitably connected.
22. A guide to the share participation laws was prepared by Kayhan Research Associates, *Share Participation* (Tehran: Kayhan Research Associates, 1976).
23. Graham, op. cit., p. 95.
24. In 1976, there were 700 trade unions in Iran employing about 2,500 officials. Around 400,000 workers are also in cooperatives, which help to get cheaper food, housing, or credit. See *Iran Almanac, 1976*, p. 353. Fred Halliday, *Iran: Dictatorship and Development* (London: Penguin, 1979), chap. 7, describes the history of the trade union movement in Iran and relates how, under the Shah, workers' organizations were prevented from becoming an autonomous force.
25. See J. de Givry and J. Scoville, "Labor Legislation: Practice and Theory," working paper no. 9, for *Employment and Incomes Policies in Iran* (Tehran: International Labor Organization, 1973).
26. In this regard, it is interesting to note that *Iran: Who's Who: 1976* (Tehran: Echo of Iran Press, 1976), classes union leaders as "social personalities."
27. For discussions of factors that influence choice of technology; see C. Peter Timmer et al., *The Choice of Technology in Developing Countries* (Cambridge, Mass.: Harvard University Press, 1975).

II

INTERNAL LABOR MARKETS: ORGANIZATIONS AND HLM CAREERS

4

ORGANIZATIONS IN IRAN

In the course of an organization's history, employment expansion and diversification of products and product lines necessitate changes in the task structure (jobs within the organization) and social structure (relationships among organizations members). These elements shape the personnel policies affecting the careers of HLM. How quickly and in what ways an organization will adapt depend upon its members' perceptions of the surrounding circumstances and their capabilities and desires. In this sense, the entrepreneurs or manager-owners of the modern industrial enterprises in Iran were the organizational protagonists with the most power to influence internal organizational arrangements.

But the demand for efficient organizational performance as arranged by the Iranian manager-owners was limited by a number of factors from the outset. First, the licensing regulations and the absence of financial institutions to evaluate and encourage new products created monopolistic conditions in the product market and, through restrictions of entry, an entrenched industrial elite, powerful because of their wealth and/or political connections. Organizationally speaking, the lack of competition implied that entrepreneurs had few incentives to institute change, that is, to upgrade products, develop technological innovations, or implement new personnel policies that would improve productivity and further market penetration for Iranian-made goods.

Second, traditional social values formed the basic outlook of Iranian owner-managers. These values were reinforced by the political system of the Shah. Fear of reprisals from laws that were not fairly administered or fully understood, combined with the extensiveness of the Shah's information and intelligence network, generated strong feelings of distrust, insecurity, and cynicism within the industrial elite.[1] Because of these feelings, the employers were given to perceive that the organizations most suited to their own self-interests were those that kept confidential information and decision-making power within a closed circle of trusted, personal associates. This naturally had repercussions limiting the authority of most of the HLM defined in this study.

In view of the importance of organizational behavior for the utilization of HLM, five firms in the private industrial sector are examined in detail in this chapter. Given that the private sector must compete for HLM with the government-controlled establishments, a comparison between the government and private organizations using case material from two public sector industrial establishments, two civil service organizations, and a university is also undertaken.[2]

FIVE MANUFACTURING FIRMS IN THE PRIVATE SECTOR

The five firms in the sample all manufactured consumer durables and were representative, by nature of their types of products and size (all employed over 1,000 persons), of the kind of modernization effort in industry that had been actively encouraged by the government of the Shah.[3] Table 4.1 compares the five establishments, which have been given letter assignations for easy identification. In particular, Firms A, B, C, and D manufactured transport equipment, such as cars, trucks, and so on. This industry had been given special attention by the Shah, which in its entirety included 14 firms.[4] Firm E manufactured electrical machinery, primarily household appliances. The different nature of the products produced by Firm E placed it within a different competitive environment. On this point, therefore, Firm E offers a useful point of contrast to the other four firms.

All five firms, however, had equivalent technology in that they all utilized assembly line, mass production methods. The similarity in production methods permits control of the technology variable for purposes of interorganizational analysis. The presence of the same technologies, it may be hypothesized, also accounted for the fact that the percentage of HLM in all the organizations was relatively constant.[5]

Differences in size (Firm A was significantly larger), age (Firm E was the oldest), and ownership (Firm D was a joint foreign-Iranian venture) are other useful points of contrast. Finally, all these establishments were located in Tehran, which means that they operated under similar supply constraints.

Organizational Growth

A great deal of history often contributed to the status in the 1970s of the sample firms. The major shareholder in Firm A, for example, began as a dealership for foreign products, then as a small mechanic's workshop that assembled a handful of auto units a week. Firm C, though begun only in 1965, was preceded by an unsuccessful attempt by its founders' forefathers to set up the same kind

The Shah Still Lives 91
April 91

TABLE 4.1

Comparison of the Private Manufacturing Firms in Sample

Company	Industry	Number of Employees	Percent of HLM	Location	Date Founded (age in 1976)	Ownership and Licenses	Basic Technology	Degree of Vertical Integration (percent)	Number of Product Lines
A	Transport equipment	8,500	5-6	Tehran	1962 (14)	Private Iranian venture; began share participation plan in 1976; German and English licenses	Assembly line, mass production	63 (including 20% of the parts)	5
B	Transport equipment	2,000	5	Tehran	1960 (16)	Private Iranian venture; began share participation plan in 1976; German license	Assembly line, mass production	35	1
C	Transport equipment	1,250	8	Tehran	1965 (11)	Private Iranian venture; U.S. license	Assembly line, mass production	20-30	3
D	Transport equipment	1,800	5	Tehran	1973 (3 years old since foreign partner)	Private joint U.S. and Iranian venture; U.S. partner is associated with large U.S. firm	Assembly line, mass production	Limited to some parts of chassis and interior (no specific figure given)	2
E	Electrical machinery, particularly household appliances	2,500	23% of employees are staff; no separate figures on HLM	Tehran	1937 (39 years old)	Private Iranian venture; began share participation plan in 1976; U.S., German and Italian licenses	Assembly line, mass production	20-60 (depending on product)	8

Source: Gail Cook Johnson, "Institutional Processes Determining the Behavior of High-level Manpower in Iran," Ph.D. dissertation, Massachusetts Institute of Technology, 1978, Table 3.2, p. 64.

of business in the late 1930s. Firm E, the oldest, originally began as a small machine shop. But it was not until the 1960-70s that these firms established themselves as serious entities in the new atmosphere that was created by the government's conscious policy to encourage private investment. Only then could franchise licenses from foreign companies be readily obtained. Firm E witnessed the most spectacular growth at this time.

The rapid growth permitted these firms also allowed them to accumulate sufficient capital to invest in other projects. Output had been expanded, employment increased, and product lines diversified and added.* The most significant factor of this growth, however, is that it had been accompanied by a great deal of vertical integration. Firm A, which manufactured 63 percent of the value of its products in 1976, was by far the most integrated. It had planned to achieve 100 percent integration by 1981.† The other firms had integrated to lesser degrees, although Firm E produced 60 percent of the components in some of its product lines.

Although this study is only concerned with parent firms, expansion had also broadened the total organization. Both Firm A and Firm E had formed industrial groups that included not only plants engaged in the manufacture of components for their vehicles and appliances but also other establishments specializing in banking, retail trade, or the manufacture of unrelated products. Firm C was also a major distributor for other kinds of equipment.

The amount of vertical integration and diversification was in response to market imperfections and the need to alleviate risk and uncertainty. It prevented the firm from having to be dependent upon other organizations outside its control for supplies of necessary inputs or, in the case of the groups where financial institutions were involved, to rely upon poorly developed capital markets within the home country.[6] More than most firms in the sample, for example, Firm A felt that the Iranian economy would become controlled to the extent that the government policy, which then favored the importation of needed capital goods and components, would be discarded for a policy that forced manufacturers to use Iranian suppliers. As this would inevitably create massive supply problems, the firm was anticipating the change by creating its own supply components.

The diversification of product and product lines also should not be thought of as innovations. With the exception of Firm D, backward integration was made possible because foreign firms through licensing arrangements were

---

*Table 4.1 notes that Firm B manufactured only one product. However, within this line, there were many variations.

†By 1977, however, such plans were shelved because of financial difficulties.

willing to install their own technology in Iran, which was taken as "given" by the Iranian firms.

As a result of these commitments to imported technology and firm expansion, Iranian firms were less than efficient. In Firm A, the high degree of vertical integration was so costly that it was estimated that the firm could not afford to change any component part for ten years!* The production cost of an Iranian-made refrigerator was estimated to be more than 50 percent higher than that of a foreign import.[7] This meant that Iranian firms could not compete in the export market and were limited to the domestic market, which was not large enough to merit efficient economies of scale. Indeed, the estimated excess capacity in these industries was substantial (see Chapter 2).

Firm D, however, the one multinational in the sample, did make some innovations in its technology to better suit Iranian conditions. A tour of the plant revealed, for instance, that while the main assembly line was highly automated, subsidiary operations were more labor-intensive, suggesting that at least in this case, multinationals were more adaptive than indigenous enterprises.[8] Vertical integration was also curtailed because the management respondent stated that "The size of plant that would be required to make vertical integration efficient is not merited by projected demand estimates."

The move toward vertical integration by Iranian firms therefore provided the necessary control of input supplies but sacrificed long-term product success for short-term profit. In part, this orientation stemmed from social roots of the particular entrepreneurs. In Firms A, B, and C, the founders (manager-owners) came from either the bazaar culture, where they were engaged in trade, or the land-owning class.

Given the essentially different nature of business in the bazaar and of landownership, the backgrounds of the entrepreneurs did not prepare them for effective management roles in long-term industrial enterprises. In addition, despite the support given to them by the Shah under licensing, they had reason to distrust the stability of government support which was an added incentive to make short-run profits at the expense of long-term gain. The bazaar merchants, as witnessed by the decisive role they played in the recent revolution, have always been a volatile source of opposition to the established elite, particularly when their business interests have been attacked. The landowners had been largely disenfranchised by land reform a decade earlier.† In short, Iranian entrepreneurs have been ambitious and creative but have maintained what Albert Hirschman has called the "ego-focussed image where the individual conceives

---

*This information was obtained from a foreign expert in the industry who was working for a competitor in Tehran.

†Under the initial land reform program, large landowners were allowed to keep only one village.

change as something that is open to him, essentially at the expense of the rest of society".[9]

General Organizational Relationships

The group organizational structure or vertical integration also permitted a greater number of production and administrative aspects to remain in the control of the manager-owner without delegation of decision-making responsibility beyond the family or extended kinship circle. The extended kinship system carried with it a definite order of preferences. The most desired persons, especially in finance and purchasing, were family members who possessed some credentials either through experience or education. If such people could not be recruited in sufficient numbers, intimate family friends, often having distant or indirect blood ties, were the next most preferable. In these instances, however, a stronger degree of control was recommended. In both these choices, organizational members came from the same elite social group.

Only as a last resort would professional managers who had no family connections be drafted from the outside. Organizations, in fact, often deleted a top position from its organizational plan or permitted a family member to hold more than one position if the very important positions could only be filled singly by a professional manager. The manager-owner had direct participation in all aspects of the organization.[10]

In the sample of firms, the principal owner was the managing director. In Firm C, all positions of any importance were filled by family members. In Firm E, some top positions below the managing director were filled by close family friends and persons who had long tenure with the organization. There were strict controls on those who had financial authority, and all top personnel were chosen by the managing director.

In Firms A and B, the top management was primarily staffed by a close group of friends. In the former firm, the managing director made all financial decisions. In the latter firm, the managing director also held the post of director of administration. This position controlled both financial and manpower matters.

Firm D, which was completely controlled by a staff of foreign managers, appeared to be an exception to the extended kinship system. But in many respects these managers were an elite. The foreign partner was adamant that control of all major decisions remain in the hands of the foreign personnel sent by the head office in the United States. Thus, for Iranians looking up from below, the top management circle appeared as closed to them as it did in the Iranian-managed firms.

Due to the extensiveness of the decision-making powers accorded to top management, positions lower down in the administrative hierarchy had been created almost solely for the purpose of collecting the information that was necessary for decisions. As the growth of the organizations had increased the complexity of information needs, a confusing array of hierarchical levels and grades had been developed. Figure 4.1 depicts these general organizational relationships.

As ascertained by an examination of job titles and job duties where this information was available, the lower levels were differentiated according to whether one was a chief or in charge of a general or broad function (such as chief of general administrative affairs) or chief or in charge of more specific functions (such as chief of production employment). Because positions could be formed ad hoc, and the growth of the organization could often change job demands, the numbers and kinds of job titles and duties assigned were highly unstable.

Supervisor-subordinate relationships also were not well defined. A person at the lower levels could and did report not only to those immediately above in the hierarchy but also to those higher up. Lateral communication between people in equivalent positions did not exist except at the directorship or top three levels. Finally, authority was restricted to the top levels at decreasing intensity.

The absence of lateral communication and orderly supervisor-subordinate communication flows ensured that no middle-level supervisor would have control over any facet of the organization independently of top-level managers. The kind of empire building in the middle ranks feared by the managers interviewed therefore was effectively prevented. This system of administration compares well with the example set by the Shah, who, as was explained in Chapter 3, usually assigned overlapping responsibilities to numerous persons and elicited reports on the same subject from many diverse sources.

The need for centralization also caused organizations to be developed along functional rather than divisional lines. In the case of Firm B, the functional divisions were very simple. Accounting, employment, and services fell under administration, while production, planning, inventory, and supplies fell under a second department called technical affairs. This was the firm where the managing director doubled as the director of administration. His dual role underscored the fact that the functional division or organizational structure was governed by the availability of acceptable or trustworthy personnel for top positions. In the other firms, the functional divisions were less broad and included separate departments for administration, service, sales, production, planning, finance, and purchasing.

The above analysis of organizational relationships, however, is only the general picture. Within this framework, there were degrees of differentiation. In this regard, the firms in the sample could be roughly divided into two groups. Group 1 included Firms A, B, and C. Group 2 included Firms D and E. For reasons that will be later elaborated, there was within group 2 some further differentiation. The differences were primarily due to the fact that Firm E was owned and operated by Iranians, while Firm D was partly owned and wholly managed by foreigners.

FIGURE 4.1

General Organizational Relationships

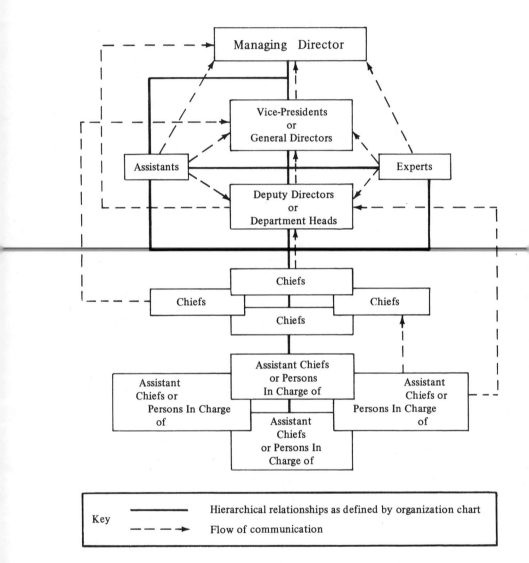

Source: Gail Cook Johnson, "Institutional Processes Determining the Behavior of High-Level Manpower in Iran," Ph.D. dissertation, Massachusetts Institute of Technology, 1978, Diagram 3.1, p. 77.

The firms in group 1 had a more personalized form of management and a less developed managerial control system. Firms B and C, for example, had no cost accounting procedures. Firm A, while having a computerized system to handle inventory, sales, production scheduling, and accounts, had been unable to make this system workable. Parts were unnumbered, and information was inaccurate and too delayed to be of use.* From remarks made by the high-level manager interviewed in this firm, the computer in the firm seemed to be there more for the prestige value it offered than for efficiency.

Group 2 firms, on the other hand, had more clearly defined organizational structures and, although their formal managerial control systems (also computerized) were, as respondents admitted, not operating to desired efficiency, they were far more advanced. In these cases, the inefficiency was more a result of a shortage of technical manpower than a lack of proper motivation or attitude on the part of the management. In short, group 2 firms typified a shift away from the extended kinship system, which stressed social relationships, to a more formalized system, which emphasized jobs or tasks over personalities. The outcome of these differences was most aptly demonstrated by the firms' policies for the recruitment, placement, training, and remuneration of HLM.

Recruitment

At the outset, the methods of recruitment that were open to Iranian employers in the private sector were limited. For instance, recourse to private employment agencies, advertisement in professional journals, and organized university drives were not feasible. Private employment agencies that specialized in recruitment and placement of manpower in permanent jobs were illegal. Despite the fact that the government did make a distinction between these types of agencies and employment subcontractors, any person wishing to set up a subcontract firm for HLM soon found that to maintain a stock of qualified manpower who were willing to be hired out at the direction of a subcontractor (as opposed to directing their own careers) was almost impossible in a labor-short economy unless in a context like the management consulting firms. Because professional journals are few in Iran and their circulation is poor, employer search through these means did not exist.

Finally, Iranian universities (unlike in the West) do not have formal procedures, such as student employment offices, to facilitate the matching

---

*Information about the computer system and how it worked was obtained from a computer technician employed in the firm. The information was unsolicite.

of graduates with employers. Employers wishing to appeal to the universities could only do so if they personally knew someone at the university whom they could ask for referrals.

Of the institutionalized employer search methods left open to the Iranian employer, many were not highly effective. The alternatives to private employment agencies were the Ministry of Labor's employment service, some management consulting firms, and more recently, organizations like the Iranian Management Association. The government employment service, however, specialized in lower levels of manpower and only occasionally would have on register the names of highly qualified Iranians living abroad who wished to be employed in Iran.

The consulting firms would accept and hold on file resumes of HLM seeking jobs. But only when another firm directly requested the consultants to recommend someone for a vacancy would they attempt to match employer and applicant. In such cases, the consulting organization's involvement in the matching process was terminated when the applicant was told to contact person X at company Y. This recruitment service, moreover, was only a very small part of the consulting firms' services.

The Iranian Management Association (IMA) started, in September 1975, a program designed to attract back to Iran qualified Iranians living abroad. As many Iranians did not return because of political difficulties and the military draft, the IMA had promised to act as a mediator between the government and the Iranian abroad to help settle these differences, and to obtain two-year contract commitments from employers before an Iranian returned. Because the government, in 1976, had made it clear that no one could be exempt from the draft, it was unlikely this program could ever be effective.

Newspapers in Iran were full of ads requesting HLM. But management consultants interviewed suggested that these ads did not get responses from as wide an area as they were designed to reach. Prospective applicants felt there was no point in answering an ad when they knew no one in the company to work on their behalf. The management respondent for Firm D, for example, complained that the firm had had no responses to an ad that had been running in both the English and Farsi dailies the week before.* If indeed the low response to newspaper ads was due to a potential applicant's perceptions of hiring procedures, newspaper advertising was only useful insofar as it indicated to those looking for work that it was worth contacting those members of their extended family who were connected with the recruiting organization for help.

---

*However, the lack of response might also have been due to the fact that the job advertised was asking for very high educational qualifications but offered a relatively low-status position.

Ultimately, Iranian employers' easiest means of recruitment were the least formal. These included direct contact with friends and relatives (indirectly through newspapers) and raiding, which was inevitable in a tight labor market. Raiding, as described by one respondent, occurred in a direct and indirect fashion. In the first instance, an employer, during the course of his outside contacts with employees in other firms, would meet a person he found particularly suitable for his organization. He would then ask the person to leave his present job and come to work for his organization at a higher salary. Many of the employees who stated that they learned of their jobs because "the employer asked them to join" could be pinpointed as possible "raids." In the indirect method, the employee initiated the move. Employees would ask for a leave of absence or vacation from their present job and go to work for a competitor. After they completed a probationary period at the second place, they would then bargain with the two employers for the better salary.

However, the lack of institutionalized employer search methods was not simply a function of government policy (as in the case of private employment services) or underdevelopment of the service sector (as in the case of universities). Institutional forms of recruitment also had not developed because there had been little demand from the majority of employers to do so.

In this study's sample of private manufacturing firms, for example, there was a notable difference between group 1 and group 2 firms. Group 1 firms employed both relatives and friends and newspapers to find HLM for the organization. But only group 2 also used other methods, such as university recruitment drives at home and abroad and the maintenance of waiting lists for applicants to which reference could be made when a position became vacant. Firms in group 1 did not have a need for waiting lists because they were more willing to create positions on demand for applicants they thought might be useful to the organization than were group 2 firms. Interviews with employees in both Firm A (group 1) and Firm E (group 2) showed that around 57 percent in Firm A compared to 31 percent in Firm E were hired through friends and relatives.

By relying upon these few search methods, group 1 firms unfairly restricted their recruitment areas. Given that all firms stressed that they experienced difficulty in getting enough qualified manpower for their HLM positions, particularly engineering and accounting positions, the pursuit of this restricted-area policy can only be justified by the fact that group 1 firms placed a higher value upon finding qualified persons who were "known" than upon finding persons who were perhaps qualified but "unknown" for all HLM levels of their organizations. This was in keeping with the extended kinship system.

With respect to who was hired by the companies, all firms without exception showed preference for graduates from foreign schools in countries where their licensor was located or from the Harvard-influenced Iranian Centre for Management Studies.

Placement

An examination of the number of positions filled by new hires in a firm relative to the number filled through promotions, particularly at the top levels, can indicate to what degree promotion opportunities for HLM exist in the organization. Even in firms with a good manpower utilization record, a certain proportion of the top management will be hired directly into their positions from the outside rather than promoted from within the organization. Unlike the situation for blue-collar occupations, some interorganizational jumping must be accepted for successful HLM. In addition, organizations within the Iranian context had to rely most heavily upon outside rather than inside recruitment to fill positions because the process of organizational growth created more HLM positions than there were people from internal sources to fill them. Notwithstanding these career and organizational aspects, however, poor promotional opportunities are indicated if the number hired to the number promoted is as great or greater at top positions as it is for positions lower down.

In group 1 firms, the friends and relatives who held top positions were almost exclusively hired from without. As these companies did not map out organizational charts to help them to plan what positions in the future would need filling, there was no clear idea as to where an employee in the company could advance. The absence of any kind of formal appraisal system also prevented the company from knowing the potential of its HLM staff. In most cases therefore an employee's social relationship with the organization members occupying superior positions was the most pertinent criterion for placement. This limited career prospects. An employee in the lower ranks could hope to advance to successive levels of chiefs if a good relationship was developed with the superiors. This rise could be meteoric, but only to a point. Less personable individuals could only expect to shift interdepartmentally with little or no promotional value attached to the jobs.

The difference between group 1 and group 2 firms was that the latter had organizational charts that were updated to reflect HLM needs for six months in the future and permitted them to groom for promotion an organizational member in advance. In addition, formal appraisal systems in all or some departments helped to pinpoint promising candidates. In this way, Firm E had the highest percentage of its top positions staffed by promotions.

In Firm D, unfortunately, the monopolization of the top positions by head office personnel greatly restricted the number of vacancies at this level that could be filled by internal promotions. The management respondent in this regard stated that there were individuals in the ranks immediately below who deserved promotion but that there were no vacancies for them. There was one Iranian who did occupy a top position. He, however, was inherited from the old organization and kept in his position because of his relationship with one of the Iranian partners. His role in actual managerial duties was kept to a low level.

Firm D's policy therefore is restrictive for those who start close to the top in the management hierarchy.* For those who begin lower down greater opportunities were available because the system allowed their potential to be noted and developed. In this respect, Firm D's policy was more favorable than those of the group 1 firms.

Management Development

In a tight labor market, turnover thresholds can be reduced through institutional arrangements only partially because a large part of turnover can be attributed solely to the economic situation. This turnover discourages investment in general training[11] and provides a rationale for the maintenance of promotion and hiring policies based upon the extended kinship system. Friends and relatives, after all, can be expected to remain employed with the organization longer than other persons. Group 1 firms stated that there were no particular training or development programs apart from those offered by the licensor as a necessary prerequisite for handling the imported technology because they felt the resulting turnover would negate the investment.

Group 2 firms, in contrast, offered formal on-the-job training in the form of job rotation to middle (in the case of Firm D) and upper (in the case of Firm E) levels of management. Job rotation has advantages in that it does contain some specific content, is not a very expensive form of manpower development, and accords well with the normal pattern of HLM careers, which habitually entails interdepartmental moves. The existence of management development programs in only group 2 firms underscored the differences in managerial philosophy and the divergence from the personalized extended kinship system.

Remuneration

Effective benefit and salary administration was plagued by a number of market imperfections. For instance, the benefits that any company had to provide, either because it was a legal requirement or an industry tradition, were so costly, averaging 50 percent again of salary costs, that none of the employers in the study had any incentive to provide benefits that, when tied to tenure, would be substantial enough to act as a deterrent to turnover.

---

*For this reason, an outside consultant whom the author interviewed recommended that this organization develop more levels in its job evaluation scheme to act as an incentive for the employees.

Companies, for example, in accordance with a 1962 labor law amendment, had to share profits with employees. The amount of the profit share was not dictated by the individual company's record but by industry affiliation. Therefore, the blanket coverage of the law restricted any incentive potential and essentially amounted to an expected annual bonus of 40 to 100 days' salary for all employees in the industry. Biased government administration of dismissal cases further increased benefit costs by awarding high termination pay settlements.

Contributions to the government social security plan had to be made and, according to management, discouraged the development of private pension plans. In addition, vacation pay, medical benefits, yearly bonuses, low-interest loans, and transportation allowances had to be provided because it was industry tradition to do so. If one decided not to provide these items, the company ran the risk of not being able to attract its share of applicants.

The absence of comparable interfirm salary data made the setting of salary levels extremely problematic. Part of the problem of salary comparisons was compounded by the fact that there were a great number of firms in the labor market that had no set standards to assess the correspondence between job duties and salary levels. As a result, there could be little equivalency between job titles in similar organizations. For example, according to employee questionnaire responses, the chiefs of production control in Firm A and Firm E both had similar education and amounts of tenure but received 95,000 rials ($1,357) and 50,000 rials ($714) per month, respectively.

In 1974, the labor market information situation had been somewhat improved. In that year, a private consulting firm offered to do comprehensive salary surveys for private firms. The surveys made careful comparative analyses of job duties, education, and experience levels for each customer. Firms A, D, and E used this service. In the case of Firm A, however, the only firm in group 1 to subscribe to the plan, results were not systematically applied.

Without accurate knowledge of the market rates, and in an atmosphere of raiding, salaries were established through individual bargaining between the employer and an applicant. For those applicants with experience who better knew the job market, employers often paid more than was necessary. New entrants to the labor market who were not as knowledgeable of the market situation often received less relative pay. The latter naturally wanted significant pay increases when they discovered the salaries of their colleagues.

The rapidly increasing level of salaries for new hires also made it difficult for employers to design and maintain salary scales. An engineer with two years' experience and a bachelor's degree in engineering, for example, could be hired in 1974 for 90,000 rials ($1,286) per month. But, in 1975 and 1976, an engineer with similar qualifications had a hiring rate of 120,000 rials ($1,714) and 140,000 rials ($2,000) per month, respectively. Given that an effective salary policy rewards those with longer tenure better than those with shorter tenure, position

FIGURE 4.2

Comparison of Average Salary Costs Using Two Systems for a Company

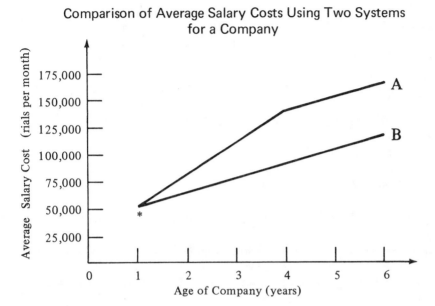

*The diagram assumes that in year 1 all persons had to be hired. A: Average salary cost with equitable salary scales. B: Average salary cost that does not adjust existing salaries to salaries paid for new hires.

Source: Gail Cook Johnson, "Institutional Processes Determining the Behavior of High-Level Manpower in Iran," Ph.D. dissertation, Massachusetts Institute of Technology, 1978, Table 3.2, p. 100.

and qualifications being equal, this would mean that the salary for the engineer hired in 1974 would have had to be increased by at least 33 percent in 1975 and by at least an additional 16 percent in 1976. Similarly, the salary for an engineer hired in 1975 must have been increased by 16 percent in 1976. These percentages are only minimums because they do not account for promotion or merit increases or reflect payment for the additional experience gained by prolonged employment with the company.

As vacancies for any level were always being created by organizational growth, normal attrition, and job shifts, the number these organizations had to hire from the labor market each year was never zero. For an employer therefore who was only conscious of the dollar costs of the total salary bill and who had no realization of the intangible costs related to turnover, it appeared cheaper to keep hiring new manpower than it was to try to retain the old by keeping equitable salary scales. This relationship is demonstrated in Figure 4.2.

Given that in group 1 firms the most important high-level positions were filled by trusted relatives, turnover in other administrative positions was not considered crucial, providing personnel could be recruited from outside to fill vacancies. In group 2 firms, however, organizational members were considered from the point of view of their promotability and therefore turnover levels were monitored. Thus it is not surprising that in group 1 firms salary levels were inversely related to tenure, while in group 2 firms those with highest tenure, all else equal, were paid more. Comparison of average salary levels in Firm A, for example, showed that those with three years' or more tenure received at least 2 percent less pay than those with less than three years' tenure (positions equal), while in Firm E persons of equal position with three years' or more tenure received almost 15 percent more than their less tenured counterparts.

Both group 2 firms had formal job evaluation schemes and utilized the interfirm salary survey to revise salary levels in line with market rates. The institution of job evaluation programs in group 2 firms created salary structures that were radically different from those in group 1 firms in more than just the tenure-salary question. The formal evaluation system accorded most reward to one's job duties and, secondarily, awarded higher benefits for education and experience. This process defined clear salary ranges for all positions in a hierarchical order.

The informal nature of salary-setting policies in group 1 firms, on the other hand, created disparities not only within levels of the organization but also among levels of the organization. A very small proportion of one's salary was attribted to position alone. For example, one respondent in Firm A who earned a total of 175,000 rials ($2,500) per month received only 25,000 rials ($357) of this as position pay.

The individual bartering system permitted individual characteristics to be most highly rewarded, and created situations whereby persons with more education, experience, and/or social connections got paid more than someone in a higher position. While this policy is consistent with the personalized nature of hiring and promotion procedures in group 1 firms, it created a great deal of discontent. Firm A stated that it tried to get around this by keeping within minimum and maximum ranges of salary offers, while, at the same time, rewarding more those with the best bargaining positions in other ways, such as living allowances.

Group 1 versus Group 2

This discussion of personnel policies has demonstrated that group 2 firms, Firms D and E, had more consciously developed manpower policies than group 1 firms, Firms A, B, and C. The most obvious explanation for these differences was that Firms D and E had managements who possessed greater managerial experience. In Firm D's case, the management had been able to institute policies developed by the head office and subsidiaries around the world.

Firm E, conversely, had gained experience over time. Since its inception 39 years ago, Firm E had to adjust to less favorable economic conditions of the pre-1960s era and to face the inevitable breakdown of complete family control because the family members were becoming more diversified in their interests or too old to carry on the full-time management of the firm in the future.

The industry of which it was a part was more competitive than the industry of the other firms. Firm E, for example, manufactured products that cost between $100 and $200. Due to the fact that Iranian industry did not make products of equal quality to foreign counterparts, a consumer would consider paying the high import duties to buy a foreign import at the inflated cost of $300 to $600. On the other hand, the basic cost for a product in group 1's and Firm D's industry was $4,000 to $20,000 and consumers would well think twice before they paid $12,000 to $60,000 for the additional quality.

In short, the challenge created by the circumstances governing Firm E had inevitably developed a stock of abler managers who could better appreciate information control systems and the need to create a management base within the company.

In many ways the experience gained by Firm E was more pertinent in the long run than the imported experience of Firm D. The latter firm had not entirely adapted to the Iranian situation, and its unwillingness to reconsider some policies caused many of its manpower problems. The lack of vacancies into which persons could be promoted because the foreign partner insisted upon its management prerogative was such a case. Firm E, on the other hand, was under-developed more because the adaptation stage was yet incomplete.

Age, in this respect, was the key to change. Peter M. Blau, for example, found that "opposition to change in the organization, while apparently indicating perfect accommodation to existing conditions, is actually the result of insufficient adaptation to them. New comers, who had not yet become adapted, as well as less competent officials, felt threatened by change."[12] "This suggests that an organization's concept of the optimum rate of change is a function of past experience, and that acceleration of change, not velocity of change, is the central variable which evokes resistance (to change)."[13]

The younger organizations, therefore, such as Firms A, B, and C, had not had the time or gained sufficient experience to develop organizational procedures significantly different from those they had at the beginning. Their foundation in the prosperous 1960s had not challenged them enough to seek change. Their personal style of administration was typical and was reflected in the organizational prototypes established by the government. For this reason, comparison with government organizations is important.

GOVERNMENT ORGANIZATIONS

There are two main types of government organizations: the civil service administration and industrial enterprises. The Iranian government had taken responsibility for the extraction and production of primary inputs that required investment in high-level technology. These industrial enterprises differed from others in Iran in that the government and not private concerns had majority control, despite the high participation of foreign manpower within them.

The National Iranian Oil Company (NIOC) and National Iranian Steel Industries Company (NISCO) are perhaps the most notable examples of government-controlled industrial enterprises. Connected to NIOC are a number of wholly owned subsidiaries. Within the military sphere, the Military Industries Organization (MIO) was an umbrella for organizations dealing with electronics, ordnance, and vehicle assembly and maintenance. With respect to this study, information about organizations and personnel policies was gathered on two civil service organizations, NIOC, and an electronics firm connected to MIO.

The private firms were differentiated according to their recruitment and placement policies, manpower development programs, and salary administration. The key to the differences was informality versus formality. In this sense, government organizations appear to be essentially different from group 1 firms. Levels and positions in the bureaucracies were clearly defined for the permanent civil service. The government was the major employer and, as a result, a significant number of employees were hired through means other than the extended kinship system.

The government, moreover, was better able to support and justify for social reasons investment in general training. Many government employees were sent abroad to obtain postgraduate degrees, provided they worked for the government two years for every year they were supported. The free education program in Iranian institutions of higher education (mentioned in Chapter 2) increased this investment in general training.

The government organizations also were not bounded by the labor laws of the private sector. They had therefore been able to design benefit policies that were tied to tenure. An employee with the government, for example, received a full pension after 20 years of service. Substantial housing loans could be obtained by individuals with a certain amount of tenure at very low interest rates. The government also had well-defined salary scales for its civil servants that accorded set amounts for position, education, experience, and tenure.

The actual administration of the personnel policies contrasted sharply, however, with the principles outlined above. As mentioned in Chapter 3, government organizations were staffed at the top by political appointees. It was in these persons' interest to prevent delegation of authority and to maintain the extended kinship system among the top levels of their bureaucracies. In other words, empire building was as prevalent in the civil service as it was in the private sector at top levels.

In both civil service organizations studied, the heads of the organizations were the sole arbiters for all disputes and made all decisions. The director of one or the organizations in fact had tried unsuccessfully to combat custom by delegating authority. He was severely criticized for this practice. In this organization, a web of family connections that extended back through many previous directorships could be traced. A previous director, for example, during the course of his tenure, had staffed all the top positions with his brothers, sisters, and cousins. Others in the organization in 1976 held their high positions because of social connections elsewhere in the government.

Obtaining educational qualifications abroad with government support also did not guarantee promotions to higher positions. Two persons in one civil service organization, in fact, related that they had been demoted when they returned from their studies. Others frequently met with an impasse early in their careers that prevented promotions to positions for which they felt they were qualified. In the other civil service organization, respondents stated that "promotions to a certain level occurred as a matter of course, but promotions beyond this level were very difficult unless one had connections."

The consultant for the National Iranian Oil Company explained that top positions in the company are occupied by the political appointees and then by foreigners. Iranian engineers or technocrats in the company, therefore, were never allowed to progress to the position of project manager. Rather, they were shifted laterally among departments and divisions within NIOC.

A similar atmosphere was noted to exist in the MIO firm studied. The central philosophy of the firm was stated to be management-by-objectives. However, the philosophy was not operational, the management respondent reasoned, because "there is a great resistance to delegating authority and a distinct belief that more people makes for better efficiency. . . . The managing director is deferred to for the final decision on everything. The organizational chart is a myth despite the lip service paid to it." The respondent went on to describe how there was a great deal of favoritism, creation of superfluous positions to be filled by personal friends, and contradiction of established rules. This scenario is certainly reminiscent of group 1 firms' policies.

The administration of salaries in the government service organizations was perhaps the most telling example of the state of manpower policy within the government. Despite the fact that the government had set salary scales, they accorded the highest percentage of a salary rating to one's education, experience, and tenure and the least part to hierarchical positions, except at the very highest levels. By this method, a person with long tenure could earn more than a new hire in a higher position. Similarly, like persons in group 1 firms, persons with more education earned considerably more than others in the same position with the same tenure. The consultant for NIOC also commented upon the existence and unfairness of this system at NIOC.

Favoritism also played a part in how benefits were awarded among the personnel. In civil service organizations, persons could have radically different amounts of take-home pay because of the extra benefits accorded to them. At the discretion of the department heads, employees could be given large amounts for overtime work and "padasht" (special project pay). Persons working on the same project and in the same capacity, for instance, were given very different amounts of padasht. For department heads and above who could not qualify for overtime pay, the superiors were given large, unaudited slush funds that could be disposed of among their subordinates as they saw fit.[14]

Other serious discrepancies also existed. Benefits were higher in the public sector than in the private sector, in part because government salaries were substantially lower than those in the private sector.* These remained a factor even after benefits were accounted for. Thus highly sought-after individuals who were willing to forego long-term benefits for short-term gain in salaries, and who would refuse to work for the government at the regular salary levels, were hired by the directors of the government organizations as consultants. These positions were not part of the official civil service ranks. As a consequence, they could be paid high salaries, set by individual bargaining, without any benefits. Employees in the civil service organizations felt a great deal of resentment toward the consultants because they saw no reason why these persons should get such high salaries. Their job duties were essentially the same.

A bulletin from the *Iran Economic Service* summarized the government situation:

> On 4th of February, 1975, the daily *Ayandegan* noted that two more senior executives of government enterprises had left for the private sector. . . . Government jobs should not be allowed to become less attractive; nor the undemocratic spirit of government bureaucracy with its favoritism and discriminations . . . allowed to continue.
>
> . . . The situation has been made even more complicated by the considerable disparity and chaos in government pay scales. In a state-own bank whose annual credit volume and lending capacity is in excess of 20,000 million rials ($286 million), the second top executive draws a monthly salary of less than 100,000 rials ($1,429) a month. Yet, under him he has employed banking specialists (consultants) who are not older than the number of years he has worked for the bank, but who receive double his salary.

---

*NIOC was not obliged to follow government pay scales, but, since the early 1970s, it pursued a policy of low wages and salaries.

In many instances, government agencies have been forced to offer new graduates of medical and engineering colleges salaries which even a deputy minister does not dream of. At the same time there are tens of thousands of doctors, engineers, judges, teachers, etc., who cannot make ends meet on their government pay, and are just waiting for an opportunity to leave government service.[15]

Low government salaries and poorly devised personnel policies have not only encouraged turnover among the most able government servants but have also created poor morale among those remaining in the civil service. This attitude has been particularly engendered by unfavorable comparisons of one's pay and position to others considered of equal ability.* Thus it is not surprising that in an unsuccessful attempt to curtail strikes by HLM in NIOC and the administrative civil service, the Iranian government in 1978 offered salary increases of 40 to 100 percent.[16] By this time, injustices were already too keenly felt. For Iranian technocrats within NIOC, the blockage of promotion channels by foreigners had been an additional source of frustration that government measures failed to address.

Moreover, low pay also fostered a great deal of multiple jobholding. Many of the educated Iranians in the civil service were part-time university professors. One employee interviewed, in fact, stated that he taught 18 hours a week until last year. Many others ran trading firms, small businesses, or free-lanced in their professions. In this regard, a businessman recited how he went to see an official at NIOC who was interested in the man's product. When he asked the official what contractual agreements NIOC was prepared to make, the main looked very surprised and said, "This is not for NIOC but for my own company!"

The government seemed to ignore these activities. There was, for instance, no conflict of interest laws. It was not unusual for an employee's company to get a contract with the very government organization he worked for. In these cases it was not clear that the government did not know who was the head of the contracted firm.

Quite apart from the implied dispersion of interests and energies multiple jobholding fostered, it offered an outlet for disgrunted spirits. When one civil servant, for example, was asked why he didn't quit his government job to run his much more lucrative import business full time, he replied, "If I did that I would have to rent an office and buy all my own office supplies and equipment as well as lose easy access to many of my customers. Besides, my government

---

*Other types of incidences plague lower-level employees. For example, in March 1975, tea servants in one civil service organization who had secondary school diplomas had their salaries reduced by $43 per month. Only after they banded together to protest the action was their previous salary level reinstated.

salary and pension is my share of the oil money! They can't possibly expect me to live on it!''

INSTITUTIONS OF HIGHER EDUCATION

Due to the importance of the education system, a final note about the institutions of higher education should be added. In 1976, the starting salary for a university instructor with a bachelor's degree was 50,000 rials ($714) per month at the University of Tehran.[17] A full-time tenured professor with a doctoral degree received 120,000 rials ($1,714) per month at the same university. Both these salaries were far below the private sector rates usually offered for similar educational qualifications, despite the fact that these figures reflected substantial increases in recent years. Full Iranian professors, moreover, in the university that was studied for this project, received less pay than both foreign professors with the same qualifications and most of the part-time instructors. Further, because professors were offered no extra pay for research, little research in the universities was done.

Thus attachment to the institutions of higher education was generally minimal, and the majority of full-time university professors held other jobs as well. The result was that a good academic environment was lacking. Poor personnel administration in Iran therefore affected not only the organizations that hired the products of the Iranian educational system for careers in the industrial environment but also had adverse impact on one of the roots of the social system, the institutions of higher education.

CONCLUSIONS

This chapter has shown how the existence of the extended kinship system had affected organizational development and personnel policies in Iran. The primary emphasis has been on a sample of firms that were representative of consumer durable industries, industries that were one of the cornerstones of Iran's economic development. However, evidence from radically different organizations, such as the government civil service, suggested that the extended kinship system was alive and well in the vast majority of organizations in Iran, regardless of sector affiliation.

Under central government authority via the functioning of licensing, the modern industrial sector had grown to include a number of large private establishments that were the result of vertical expansion. By protecting the handful of entrepreneurial elite through the establishment of monopolistic conditions, government policy had sacrificed innovation for uncertain growth in the number of product lines and goods and services under the auspices of these industrial groups.

The lack of competitiveness in the product market did not encourage employers to be cost-conscious. As a result, organizations were unaware of the indirect costs attached to the recruitment, and turnover, of their manpower. In addition, they were not cognizant of the value of the training employees received simply in the course of performing their job duties, that is, informal on-the-job training. In the absence of knowledge about these more subtle costs and benefits, the employers only realized the astronomical costs of hiring salaries (and therefore the prohibitive direct costs to effective salary administration; see Figure 4.2), the futility of investment in general training programs, and the difficulty of retaining the majority of their HLM for any period of time because of the highly competitive situation in the manpower market.

The employers therefore perceived that the preservation of the extended kinship system was of great importance. It provided the source of the most reliable and stable HLM. Friends and relatives could also be counted upon to keep the confidence of the employers, a necessity required by the Shah's divide and conquer style of rule.

Within the private sector, the expansion of organizations vertically was rationalized not only on the basis of correcting for market imperfections but also as a means to centralize operations under a trusted kinship circle.

The similarity between the managerial practices of the private industrialist and those of the government administrator are not surprising. Both were trying to protect their power position in an environment that made them feel insecure and watchful. The preservation of the extended kinship system was also a conditioned social response. When writing about the Shah's investments abroad for example, Robert Graham noted that, "Interestingly, those [international companies] which appealed most to the Shah nearly always involved companies that were family-controlled or run by a powerful figure."[18]

In brief, the existence of the extended kinship system created organizations that did not utilize the potential of Iran's scarcest resource—HLM. Decision making was very centralized. Job duties and functional divisions within the organizations, that is, the division of labor, were governed by the supply of friends and relatives rather than by the dictates of organizational needs or economies.

In the government sector, recruitment methods were more varied and training investments more prevalent, as was necessitated by the government's role in upgrading the skills of the general populace. But in both the public and private sectors, the allocation of manpower, that is, promotions and the position into which one is hired, was highly dependent upon one's personal relationship with the decision making authority.

Moreover, in both sectors, incentive structures were devised in such a way that ability and job performance were the least rewarded. Within the civil service the inability to offer monetary rewards to the full-time civil servant equal to those in the private sector and to private consultants or foreigners brought into the organizations created a toleration for multiple jobholding both within and outside the government and, ultimately, labor unrest.

The exception to the general picture was the group 2 firms, Firm D and Firm E. Both had more formalized policies that attempted to pinpoint, develop, and reward expertise within the organization. The difference between the group 2 firms and the group 1 organizations (Firms A, B, and C) can be largely accounted for by their different historical backgrounds.

Despite the fact that Firm D and Firm E had benefited from recent economic conditions and the government licensing policies, the former was managed by foreigners who drew upon the experience of the head office in the United States and the latter began in an environment that did not benefit from either the boom conditions of the 1960s or the extensive patronage of the government. In 1976, Firm E was also witnessing the demise of its founding family. Group 1 firms, on the other hand, were managed by Iranians and their present organizations began in response to the favorable atmosphere of the 1960s. In Iran's consumer durable industry, most firms began at that time.

The fact that Firm D's policies stop short of permitting anyone not from the parent organization in the United States from rising to the top levels of management suggests that foreign management control in Iran was ultimately detrimental to the development of human resources. Unless Iranians were trained to assume top responsibilities, the autonomous development of Iranians became very limited. In this sense, the initial efforts by Firm E to institute formal personnel practices were a more meaningful step. The foreign firms' major contribution was toward developing manpower at lower and middle management levels.

The impact of the extended kinship system must naturally undergo further empirical investigation if it is indeed to be shown as a highly pertinent factor for HLM. Such an examination is the task set out in Chapter 5.

NOTES

1. Marvin Zonis, *The Political Elite of Iran* (Princeton, N. J.: Princeton University Press, 1976), found that these feelings formed the basic orientations of the elite in Iran.

2. Data from the five private manufacturing firms were collected between May and September of 1976 using an in-depth, open-ended interview with a top organizational official. The interview lasted two to four hours, covered such topics as organizational history and structure, recruitment, and placement and development of HLM, and generally included a tour of plant facilities. This outline was also to be used as a basis for an International Labor Organization high-level manpower survey in Iran. The outline is reputed to be the one used by Mark Blaug et al. in their study *The Utilisation of Educated Manpower in Industry: A Preliminary Report* (London: Oliver and Boyd, 1967). (The ILO team members in subsequent meetings were indecisive about whether their high-level manpower project would be completed.) Interviews were complemented by structured interviews with a selected sample of HLM in the organization who were asked about personal background,

career, and job-related factors. In the case of the civil service organizations and the university, information was obtained by participant observation and interviews with employees. Within government-controlled industrial enterprises, information was considered more confidential and thereby harder to obtain. In one case, an interview relating to manpower policies was permitted, but discussion of technology or products was not permitted. In another, information was obtained indirectly through a consultant assigned to study HLM problems in the organization. He unsuccessfully tried to have the author admitted to the establishment. For a more comprehensive discussion of interview outline and methods of entry into organizations, see Gail Cook Johnson, "Institutional Processes Determining the Behavior of High-Level Manpower in Iran," Ph.D. dissertation (Cambridge, Mass.: Massachusetts Institute of Technology, 1978).

3. From the point of view of product diversification, it would have been appropriate also to study such industries as foodstuffs, detergents, and textiles. In all cases, admittance was refused or prevented by last-minute organizational difficulties. A meeting arranged with the managing director of a textile firm, for example, was canceled at the last moment because of a major argument between the founding partners. Admittance was refused outright at a food manufacturer, soft drink bottler, and cement manufacturer. There is no way to tell how different these organizations may be from the ones studied. To the extent that these industries have had a longer history and must contend with different market influences, notable differences with the private firms studied might have been found. The five industries in the sample, can, however, be assumed to represent mass production, assembly line industries for consumer durables. See ibid.

4. "The Future of the Automobile Industry," *Iran Economic Service*, no. 23 (March 4, 1975), 2-4, lists the firms in this industry.

5. J. Woodward, *Industrial Organization: Theory and Practice* (London: Oxford University Press, 1965), studied how various technologies can affect organization structure and manpower requirements.

6. For a discussion of the effects of market imperfections upon industrial organization, see G. B. Richardson, "Organization of Industry," *Economic Journal*, September 1972; and Oliver E. Williamson, "The Vertical Integration of Production: Market Failure Considerations," *American Economic Review*, May 1971. For discussion of Iran specifically, see Peter Richardson, "Business Policy in Iran," *Journal of General Management* (forthcoming).

7. Ibid.

8. Gerard K. Boon, "Technology Choice in Metal Working, with Special Reference to Mexico," in *Technology and Employment in Industry: A Case Study Approach,* ed. A. S. Bhalla (Geneva: International Labor Organization, 1975), discovered similar behavior with a multinational company in Mexico.

9. Albert O. Hirschman, *The Strategy of Economic Development* (New Haven, Conn: Yale University Press, 1967), p. 23.

10. In Firm A, for example, the author was told by an employee that the managing director and owner of the firm would go to the end of the assembly line to place a large wad of bills on a shelf and announce to the workers: "You can divide this money among yourselves if I see by the end of the day X number of cars come off the line." This was his direct involvement with improving production. During interviews with top company officials, it was also not unusual for these executives to be interrupted at 10-minute intervals by production employees asking permission to go to the dentist or for some other minor decision. Richardson, op. cit., p. 12, also says that in one firm he studied "the businessman who has major interests in forty companies still selects management for each. His brother signs all

cheques with a value of over $1,000; and any major product design must go to him for approval."

11. See Gary Becker, *Human Capital* (New York: National Bureau of Economic Research, 1964).

12. Peter M. Blau, *The Dynamics of Bureaucracy* (Chicago: University of Chicago Press, 1955), p. 197.

13. W. H. Starbuck, *Organizational Growth and Development* (London: Penguin, 1971), p. 45.

14. Robert Graham, *Iran: The Illusion of Power* (New York: St. Martin's Press, 1978), p. 163, suggests that the slush fund for end-of-year bonuses to all civil service organizations came from the Pahlavi Foundation. NIOC is a possible source of the foundation funds.

15. "Top Executive Salaries in Iran," *Iran Economic Service*, no. 21 (February 18, 1975): 11-12.

16. *New York Times*, November 28, 1978, pp. D1-D6.

17. "Baheri Bares Snags in the Educational System," *Kayhan International*, September 6, 1976.

18. Graham, op. cit., p. 114.

5

CAREER SUCCESS AND
HLM BEHAVIOR

The elitism of the Iranian social system was translated into organizational practices that were predominantly mediated by extended kinship relationships. These had significant impact for the HLM who were not members of the established elite under the Shah, such as his political appointments, the highest civil servants, and the large industrialists. The ways in which HLM have been utilized, their responses to the labor market, and their opportunities for career success represent some of the consequences of the elitist system that are examined in this chapter. The focal point of the analysis is centered upon a series of interviews with HLM.

THE HLM INTERVIEWS

Undoubtedly the number of HLM in Iran as defined for the purpose of this study is extremely large. However, empirical research in Iran is rare and the prevalence of the Shah's secret police helped to develop suspicious attitudes toward requests for information. For this reason, the goal of this study was not to query a large number of respondents but to obtain quality responses from a selected sample of between 100 and 150 HLM respondents. In this light, 117 responses to a structured interview schedule were obtained. The interviews were comprehensive and asked the respondents about general demographic information, educational background, career history with emphasis upon present and first jobs, incidence of multiple jobholdings, and family background. The English version of the interview schedule is given in the Appendix.[1]

A total of 107 respondents was selected from the five private manufacturing firms and two civil service organizations examined in Chapter 4.* They were a necessary complement to each case study and serve to define fully the organizational picture given by employers.

Small service organizations, such as modern trading establishments and computer firms, and construction firms also figured predominantly in the Iranian economy as adjuncts to the large manufacturing establishments. These organizations were not large enough to have a need to develop any comprehensive personnel strategy. Few HLM in these firms were hired, in fact, on other than a percentage of the profits basis. But they are important in that they offered an alternative career pattern to educated HLM. For this reason, the remainder of the 117 respondents are from the small service sector. Their number is admittedly far too small for any quantitative analysis, but, in conjunction with an intimate knowledge of such organizations, these responses serve to offer valuable qualitative information on this alternative career path.†

In order to facilitate discussion of career success, the respondent's first and present jobs, as well as father's job, were ranked hierarchically in order of job status. The job status relationship is based upon the assumption that there is a definable relationship between power and job position. For purposes of definition, power can be defined along six hierarchically arranged dimensions:

Dimensions of power that have characterized Middle Eastern [and Iranian] sociopolitical patterns are the following: (1) exchange transactions where one convinces others to accede to his wishes by rewarding them for doing so (i.e., the power to reward); (2) decisional situations where one controls the decision-making environment and thus the decisions made therein; (3) debt-inflicting relationships where one does favors for others with expectation they will someday be returned; (4) overt deference behavior that gains trust and thus builds vulnerability into the temporarily more influential; (5) informational exchanges that involve the giving and withholding of information of various degrees of accuracy and importance; and (6) bargaining relationships which rest upon the bluff, the rumor, and the misrepresentation. [2]

---

*Some control was attempted in selecting the employees to be interviewed. In general, employers agreed to a selection of employees from each position level and from each department, such that the percentage of the interview sample by position and department reflected percentages of the actual population. But in no instance would the employers allow the author to pick the actual employees to be interviewed. They also limited the number of interviews to be conducted. In one case, this resulted in a very few responses.

†This intimate knowledge was gained through in-depth and informative interviews with personnel in these sectors who were met through social or business contacts in the course of living in Iran. As such, the information was not through the most academic of approaches but serves for valuable discussion.

The rise of modern industry in Iran undoubtedly has created a demand for new job skills that, in the more traditional exonomy, did not exist. However, researchers in Iran have stressed the continuity of power positions between traditional and modern Iran, so that in the final analysis while updated in terms of educational and technical knowledge requirements, the positions occupied by the new generation correspond well with those held by their fathers a generation before.[3]

Figure 5.1 outlines the job status ranks used in this study. For the most part, rankings follow those found in the private organizations studied in Chapter 4 (see Figure 4.1). Additions include consideration for the father's job position.[4]

Examination of the responses shows that the sample is composed entirely of middle-class individuals, with around 50 percent occupying positions at the level of chiefs. These persons come from predominantly middle-class backgrounds, as evidenced by father's job status. Moreover, they are well educated with none possessing less than secondary education and most (72.4 percent) having a university degree or better. Fully 41.9 percent of the respondents were educated abroad.[5] Thus, despite the fact that the definition used for HLM relates to occupation rather than to education, there appears to be a high correlation between HLM job and university education.

DETERMINANTS OF CAREER SUCCESS

It is difficult to assess career success that is, job status, on a normative plane without some basis for comparison. This is particularly so when one considers the fact that family background or the kinship relationship is sociologically important in every nation. Differences are indeed a matter of degree. Peter Blau and Otis Duncan developed a model to examine the determinants of career success in the United States.[6] The model specifies a system of causal relationships among five variables: present job status, first job status, level of education, father's job status, and father's educational level. The small sample size used here makes definitive statements of relationships difficulat, but comparison of the Blau-Duncan results with results from the Iranian HLM data using the same model is nonetheless suggestive of the varying impact of education, career precedents, and family background upon ultimate career success.

The method of analysis employed by the Blau-Duncan model is called path analysis. Path analysis is a method that permits analysis of a set of linear relationships among a number of variables in such a way as to capture not only the direct impact of one variable upon another but also its indirect impact, assuming that a causally closed system of relationships between the variables can be prescribed.[7]

FIGURE 5.1

Job Status Measurement

Class	Job Status Rank	Power-Job Position Groups
Upper Class or Elite	1	Owner-managers (private); cabinet appointments
	2	Vice-presidents, general directors (private), deputy ministers and top government administrators
	3	Self-employed professionals and merchants of industrial products
	4	Professionals working directly with persons described in code 2
Middle Class	5	Deputy directors, department heads (private and government)
	6	Professionals working under persons described in code 5
	7	Chiefs of subdepartments (government and private)
	8	Assistant chiefs and persons in charge of (government and private)
	9	Small independent merchants and proprietors in consumer trade
Worker or Peasant Class	10	"Nasaqdars" and small farmers who own their own land
	11	"Khushnishins" (agricultural laborers)

Note: The scale is ordinal in that it does specify which positions are higher or lower than others; but it does not specify the distance between categories. Also, it is not exhaustive, but includes only those job groups pertinent to this study.

Source: Gail Cook Johnson, "Institutional Processes Determining the Behavior of High-Level Manpower in Iran," Ph.D. dissertation, Massachusetts Institute of Technology, 1978, Diagram 4.1, p. 127.

Table 5.1 and Figure 5.2 compare correlation coefficient tables and data path coefficients, respectively, for the Iranian and Blau-Duncan data. Correlation coefficients indicate the degree to which variation or change in one variable is related to variation or change in the other. Path coefficients indicate the strength of the direct effects of the independent variable upon the dependent variable. Table 5.2 summarizes the results for the Iranian data and gives the measure for the indirect effects.

As is evident from Figure 5.2, present job status is assumed to be influenced directly by first job status, level of education, and father's job status and indirectly by father's level of education. First job status, in turn, is directly influenced by level of education and father's job status and indirectly by father's level of education. Level of education is influenced directly by both father's job status and father's level of education. No causal relationship is posited between father's level of education and father's job status.[8]

Difference in Impact of Father's Level of Education

In Table 5.1 some striking contrasts can be noted between the Iranian and Blau-Duncan results. First, father's level of education has much less impact upon present job status, first job status, and respondent's level of education than it has for the U. S. results. The relationships for the Iranian case are, in fact, small enough to be ignored. The difference can be construed to indicate the radically different stages of educational development existing between the two cultures.

In the United States the formal educational system has been established for many decades. As a result, formal educational qualifications have been used as a criterion for job placement not only for the present generation but also for the past generation. In that fathers influence their children to achieve an education at least as beneficial to the labor market as their own (the socialization factor), the high correlation between father's and child's educational attainments in the United States is not surprising.

Conversely, in Iran, the emphasis upon formal educational qualifications became important only as a result of the modernization effort, which brought with it an introduction to technology and large organizations. Prior to the 1930s, in fact, educational institutes that granted diplomas and degrees in secular subjects were practically nonexistent in Iran. The educational system consisted of the maktab-madrasehs, or traditional religious schools, where religious teachers taught students to read and write only to the extent that it benefited their understanding of the Koran. As a result, the better educated often received their training not in school but at home where they were taught by foreign tutors.

In retrospect, therefore, little correspondence between child's and father's formal educational qualifications appears to be justified. Almost 44 percent of

TABLE 5.1

Comparison of Correlation Coefficients for the Blau-Duncan Model: Results in Iran and in the United States

Iran HLM Study (1976)

	Variable				
Variable	Present Job Status	First Job Status	Respondent Education	Father's Job Status	Father's Education
Present job status	—	.731	.533	.422	.063
First job status		—	.468	.566	.083
Respondent education			—	.324	.151
Father's job status				—	.371
Father's education					—

American Occupational Survey (1972)

	Variable				
Variable	Present Job Status	First Job Status	Respondent Education	Father's Job Status	Father's Education
Present job status	—	.541	.596	.405	.322
First job status		—	.538	.417	.332
Respondent education			—	.438	.453
Father's job status				—	.516
Father's education					—

Source: For U.S. data: P. M. Blau and O. D. Duncan, *The American Occupational Structure* (New York, New York: Wiley, 1967), Figure 5.1, p. 170. For Iranian data: Gail Cook Johnson, "Institutional Processes Determining the Behavior of High-Level Manpower in Iran," Ph.D. doctoral dissertation, Massachusetts Institute of Technology, 1978, Diagram 5.1, p. 165.

FIGURE 5.2

Comparison of Path Coefficients (Beta Coefficients) for Blau-Duncan Model: Results in Iran and in the United States

A

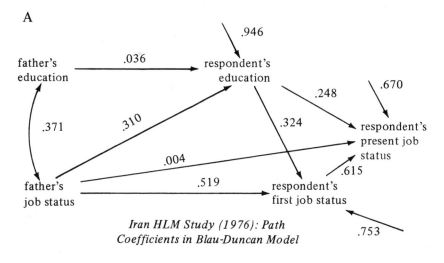

Iran HLM Study (1976): Path Coefficients in Blau-Duncan Model

B

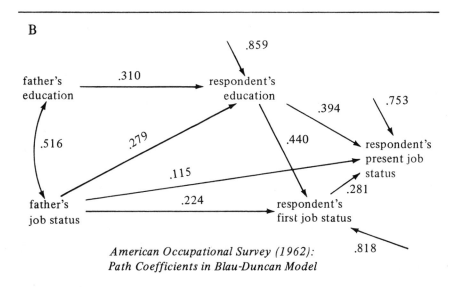

American Occupational Survey (1962): Path Coefficients in Blau-Duncan Model

Source: For U.S. data: P. M. Blau and O. D. Duncan, *The American Occupational Structure* (New York: Wiley, 1967), Figure 5.1, p. 170. For Iranian data: Gail Cook Johnson, "Institutional Processes Determining the Behavior of High-Level Manpower in Iran," Ph.D. doctoral dissertation, Massachusetts Institute of Technology, 1978, Diagram 5.1, p. 165.

TABLE 5.2

Decomposition of Variable Effects for the Blau-Duncan Model: Iranian Data

Relationship[a]		Total Correlation (correlation coefficient) (1)	Causal Effects of Independent on Dependent			Non-causal Effect (1 −(2 + 3))
Dependent Variable	Independent Variable		Direct Effects (2)	Indirect Effects (3)	Total Effect (2 + 3)	
1. Respondent's education	Father's education	.151	.151[b]	None	.151	None
2. Respondent's education	Father's job status	.324	.324[b]	None	.324	None
3. First job status	Father's education	.083	None	.049	.049	.034
4. First job status	Father's job status	.566	.519	.104	.623	−.057
5. First job status	Respondent's education	.468	.324	None	.324	.144
6. Present job status	Father's education	.063	None	.067	.067	−.004
7. Present job status	Father's job status	.422	.004	.456	.460	−.038
8. Present job status	Respondent's education	.533	.248	.199	.447	.086
9. Present job status	First job status	.731	.615	None	.615	.116

[a]The list of relationships omits any notation of a father's education-father's job status relationship because no assumption has been made about how these variables may be related causally.
[b]As these variables are not assumed in the model to have any antecedent causes, the direct effect is represented by the correlation coefficient rather than by the beta coefficient.

Source: Gail Cook Johnson, "Institutional Processes Determining the Behavior of High-Level Manpower in Iran," Ph.D. dissertation, Massachusetts Institute of Technology, 1978, Table 5.4, p. 166.

the father in the sample reported no formal educational background. The lack of relationship between these variables does not, however, mean that the socialization factor of family influence does not exist.

Difference in Impact of Respondent's Level of Education

Table 5.1 also shows that the respondent's level of education consistently exerts the most influence upon present and first job status for the U. S. data. In the Iranian data, on the other hand, the impact of the respondent's level of education upon present job status is secondary to the influence of first job status, which, in turn, is most significantly influenced not by the level of education but by father's job status. Thus, in Iran, the value of education is surpassed in importance by more subjective criteria in comparison to the United States.

Difference in Impact of First Job Status

The impact of first job status upon present job status is much stronger in Iran than it is in the United States. This difference is particularly apparent when the path coefficients between first job status and present job status in Figure 5.2 are compared. The differences clearly indicate that it is much more difficult for an Iranian to overcome early career placements than it is for someone in the United States.

Difference in Impact of Father's Job Status

Finally, comparison between the net impact of father's job status reveals the most crucial difference (see Table 5.1). In the United States, the influence of father upon children's career placement is less direct and operates most significantly through the education relationship. In other words, father's job status most highly influences a child's ability and desire to obtain educational qualifications. A father's ability to exert a force upon the U. S. child's career decreases once the child enters the labor market full time. Conversely, in Iran, the father's job status carries most impact with respect to first job status, secondarily to present job status, and only lastly to the respondent's level of education. This infers that the father's influence upon his child's career operates more through the use of personal connections than through indirect socialization processes.

Figure 5.2 further reveals that the direct impact of father's job status upon first job status is much more powerful in Iran than it is in the United States. The direct influence of father's job status upon present job status, however, is not significant in either case, but more so in the case of Iran. This again suggests that connections formed through the family are more important in Iran. If father's job status was important more from the perspective of socialization than from the perspective of connections offered by father to child, the direct impact of father's influence should persist more strongly beyond first job placement than it does simply because socialization is the more lasting influence. The indirect impact of father's job status upon present job status is very significant. Table 5.2 shows that the indirect effect of father's job status upon present career position is .456 as opposed to the direct effect of .004.

In summary, the results presented in Table 5.1 and Figure 5.2 clearly show that family influence operates in a radically different way in Iran than it does in the United States. In the latter country, family background is primarily important as a socialization factor through the influence of education. In Iran, nepotism appears to be a stronger factor. Specifically, when the spurious or noncausal effects are discounted, father's job status appears to have the most impact upon one's actual career.

According to Table 5.2, total effect of father's job status upon first job status and present job status is .623 and .460, respectively, compared to the total effect of education on first and present job status of only .324 and .447, respectively. Moreover, despite the fact that first job status upon present job status has a total impact of .615 (which is greater than the impact of father's job status upon present job status), the strength of this influence is neutralized when it is remembered that an increment of one standard deviation in father's job status fully increases first job status by an impressive .623 of a standard deviation. In other words, while education is an important determinant or precondition for career success, as evidenced by a high father's job status, family connections are essential.

The results of the Blau-Duncan model for Iran are very stable when controlled for by age.[9] But, as indicated by the high E values in Figure 5.2, the variation in the dependent variables is not fully explained by the relationships in the Blau-Duncan model. About 89 percent of the variation in respondent's level of education, almost 57 percent of the variation in first job status, and roughly 42 percent of the variation in present job status are unexplained by these relationships.* Similar results were found in the Blau-Duncan model. Clearly, additional explanations for career success must be examined, most notably the specific role played by education.

The Function of Education

With the exception of a very few individuals who are over 40 and first entered the labor market in the 1950s, before the modernization effort gathered

---

*The E values are equal to $\sqrt{1-R^2}$. The multiple R is from the regression equation in which the variable to which the E value refers is the dependent variable and all other

full momentum, all the Iranians in the sample who had job positions of department heads or above also had university degrees. But over 60 percent of the Iranians interviewed who held degrees were not classified above the level of department heads, relatively low-level jobs.* This underscores the notion that a university education was a prerequisite for favorable job placement in the modern organizations but not a guarantee despite the shortage of educated manpower.

The incidence of university-educated persons in low-status positions is partly explained by the universalization and growth of the higher educational system in Iran that has permitted persons to receive an education without the benefit of an upper-class background. James Bill, for example, relates how a 1966-67 survey of students at Tehran and National universities in Iran showed that "although the upper class is still well represented in the university system in Iran, students of non-upper-class origin are now in the definite majority."[10] Increased access to education by the lower and middle classes has been caused by the "rationalization of university entrance examination procedures [in the 1960s] whereby the prime criterion for acceptance has become merit [and] the establishment of institutions of higher education, such as Tehran Polytechnic, and training institutes and colleges (universities) attached to various government ministries."[11]

Thus the poor showing of most of the university graduates becomes more understandable. The attainment of university education independent of wealth, while undoubtedly a significant achievement for a society that heretofore gave little educational opportunity to the lower classes, did not improve initial chances in the labor market. It has been estimated that at least 50 percent of those within low-status positions are underutilized by virtue of having a university degree.†

Although the level of education does not guarantee a high level of career success, the place of education significantly influences job status, particularly for

---

variables assumed to be causally prior to it are independent variables. The percentage of the variation in the dependent variable left unexplained by the independent variables is expressed as $(1-R^2)$.

*About 25 percent of these persons were new labor market entrants. Therefore their present job status may not indicate their potential. However, as indicated above, first job status very much influences present status positions. Also see rest of chapter for discussion of why promotional opportunities are limited.

†Correspondence between occupation or job position and level of education is very difficult to assess because job experience and other forms of training can act as substitutes for formal education. With this in mind, job positions that could be conclusively assessed as requiring a certain level of education on the basis of job descriptions and judgment were so coded and matched with the actual educational level of the jobholder. In this regard, 36 percent of the job positions could not be conclusively coded as requiring a certain level of education.

initial job placements. Roughly 64 percent of those in the sample with high present job positions and 90 percent of those in high starting or first job positions (department heads or above) had Western as opposed to Iranian education.

The place of education, however, was very much influenced by family status. Almost 73 percent of the respondents with upper-middle-class backgrounds were educated abroad compared with around 27 percent of those with lower-middle-class backgrounds. This is hardly a surprising result when the financial costs of foreign education are considered, but indicates yet another area where the well-to-do place the less monied classes at a disadvantage in the labor market. Government-funded or subsidized education abroad under the Shah's regime was extended only to civil servants already working within the government or to promising students who were willing to make a commitment to work for the government after completion of their studies.[12] Thus the Iranian-educated in the private sector had the least opportunities for self-improvement through foreign education unless they were wealthy.

In conclusion, family influences affect the place of education, first job status, and to a lesser extent, respondent's level of education. As a result, career success is strongly dependent upon those factors mediated by family considerations and only secondarily by the level of education. The small sample size, however, has not readily lent itself to statistical analysis. For this reason, a qualitative examination of the evidence gathered during the course of this study offers useful insights into the careers open to HLM.

CAREER PROFILES

Of the sample of Iranian respondents, about one third had achieved some measure of career success, that is, department heads or above. The majority held lower-status jobs. From these examples, a typology of four career ladders within the middle class can be developed: the outer fringe, the organization stars, the well-connected, and the restricted movers.

The Outer Fringe

This group is called the outer fringe because its members possess characteristics that position them outside the mainstream of Iranian society. They are either foreigners or members of special ethnic groups (Jewish and Armenian).*

---

*The ethnic background of these respondents became known because respondents volunteered this information when they were being interviewed. In light of this evidence, it undoubtedly would have been useful to include a question on ethnic background in the

Under the Shah's regime, foreigners were able to work in all sectors of the economy, and as noted previously, a significant proportion was employed by the government in advisory positions. Others were employed in private manufacturing firms as technicians and managers, often in what may be termed "shadow positions," which meant that publicly the position was occupied by an Iranian who was coached by the foreigner. Foreigners also were employed and often self-employed in the modern services sector that encompassed trading firms, management consultant organizations, and professional engineering firms.

The prevalence of foreigners was naturally due to their knowledge of and experience with Western technology and customs. They were accepted with ambivalence. In terms of mobility, the self-employed foreigners were sometimes previously employed in the government or private sector, but generally they were hired for and maintained in one position in one organization.

Avenues for career success among the ethnic minorities were fewer. With the notable exception of such businessmen as Habib Elghanian, who built up a large plastics empire, few ethnic minorities have achieved great success in the private manufacturing sector. Similarly, promotion within the civil service has been difficult for these groups. The greatest opportunities for success lie within the private service sector—the traditional bazaar and its modern equivalent such as industrial trading firms.

Opportunities in other sectors of the economy have been limited for ethnic minorities partly because they have not been fully accepted by mainstream Iranians.[13] Elghanian, the Jewish industrialist mentioned above, for example, had been one of the first victims of the Shah's antiprofiteering campaign. (Under Khomeini, he was assassinated for holding Zionist sympathies.) But, most importantly, service sector employment, especially self-employment, is most promising to ethnic minorities because they have kinship connections with established persons in these sectors that they do not have elsewhere. The self-employed ethnic minorities who were interviewed, for example, either inherited their operations or had influential family contacts that aided them in starting their own trading firms.

The similarity of the occupations held by the ethnic respondents recalls Bill's comment about the homogeneity of the entrepreneurial or bourgeois class in Iran:

---

interview schedule. Such a question was omitted because it was felt that it would be too sensitive and cause respondents to be uncomfortable, to the jeopardy of the rest of the interview. In many cases, ethnic background, however, can be determined from the family name of the respondent. The Bahais have not been included in this minority group because their religion is viewed by Moslems as a heresy under Islam. Some Bahais under the Shah's regime succeeded because of proven loyalty to the Shah but their faith was underplayed. One government official, for example, who was interviewed voluntarily stated that he was a Bahai but under official pressure to declare himself a Moslem.

> [The professional middle class who are employed in large organizations] is steadily surpassing the entrepreneurial middle class in growth and importance for many reasons. In a large proportion of the developing societies [such as Iran], the bourgeois class is dominated by foreigners and minority groups. This discourages and deflects the entry of the indigenous majority who seek mobility and advancement through other channels.[14]

This does not mean that the entrepreneurial middle class is solely composed of these groups. However, the mainstream Iranians working in this sector often do so as a second job (see below) and/or as an offshoot of a primary family business that is connected to modern industrial manufacturing.

Self-employment for the ethnic minority may be preceded by employment in either the government or manufacturing sector. Tenure in the former is often, in fact, a requirement of the military draft. However, the low status of these positions, coupled with little promotional opportunities for the majority, encourages mobility to the private service sector where contacts are available.

The educational qualifications of the self-employed are indicative of the changing emphasis upon education for maintenance of class membership. The oldest minorities tend to be Iranian-educated; the younger groups often possess postgraduate degrees from U.S. universities.

The Organization Stars

This group is so named because the shared route to success was through long tenure with one organization—in either the government or the private sector. The starting position in the firm was generally low status and the organizational member was able, over time, to climb to a high-status post.

With respect to the organizational stars, in the civil service organizational attachment was usually mandatory because the government paid for their university education, which most often included postgraduate degrees from Western universities. Superior educational qualifications, however, did not always appear to be the primary justification for their promotions. In the civil service organizations that were studied, friends and relatives were instrumental in the placement and promotion of the organization stars. It was not uncommon in these instances for the proteges to receive their subsidized foreign education only after entrance to the organization. As not all government personnel who received such opportunities were equally promoted, the friendship or kinship connection appeared to be the determining factor, as performance was never accurately appraised.

The organization stars in the private manufacturing sector, at least in the organizations studied, entered the private firms with which they remained when they were either starting up during the 1960s or vastly expanding operations in the same period. The majority were middle aged (30 to 45 years of age). As such, their upwardly mobile careers were in part made possible by the fact that they were on the spot at the right time. These companies were so small in the early 1960s that it was possible to become part of a close-knit organizational core and to gain experience so that one could advance with the organization as it grew.

Many of the organizational stars' initial contact with their firms was in fact through close relations with other employees in the core firm. The others, who had no apparent personal connections with organization members at the time of hiring, possessed university degrees, albeit Iranian, in technical subjects such as mechanical engineering. The field of specialization of Iranian education did not at any other time guarantee promotional opportunities from low-status positions, but such training was undoubtedly valuable to the employer when operations were small scale, and served the new entrant well.

The organizations that employed the organization stars in the private sector had grown to such proportions and had created so many controls on behavior and additional hierarchical levels by the 1970s that persons entering the lower managerial ranks could not be as easily recognized by the executives who made promotion decisions, especially in the absence of formal performance criteria. Thus the method of advancement through long tenure with an organization appears to have become a less viable option.

The Well-Connected

The well-connected are not only well educated (most with foreign university degrees) but also have good connections. Unlike the organization stars, this group obtains foreign education independently of government support. This ability to pay for education is a consequence of their influential or wealthy backgrounds. As such, both in the private and public sectors, the well-connected entered organizations at high-status positions.*

The well-connected who began their careers in the government often experienced a great deal of organizational mobility, movement that was encouraged by both the desire to advance even higher within the civil service ranks and by politically motivated changes.

Highly placed pensioned civil servants (retirement comes after 20 years of tenure in the government) often would jump to high positions offered in the

---

*The only time the well-connected were observed to hold relatively low-status appointments was during their military draft. Even then, however, they often would be able to obtain high-level positions for the two-year draft requirement period.

private sector. In these instances, the interconnection between government and private sector patronage must be noted. Ex-civil servants, particularly if they had organizational contacts with NIOC or government organizations in charge of collecting sensitive information of a political nature, were invaluable assets to private sector ventures that operated in an unstable environment. On the one hand, they could provide better access to the necessary infrastructures and, on the other hand, could help anticipate changes in the Shah's policy.*

The well-connected who began in the private sector desired ultimately to take over the very top positions now held by close relatives or friends. As such, they could be highly mobile among enterprises associated with the parent firm but would remain within the group of organizations controlled by the parent firm.

Comparison of the organization stars with the well-connected offers some evidence as to the importance of educational background and personal connections. In the former group, respondents generally possessed either personal connections or educational qualifications of a particular sort, that is, needed technical degrees when first hired into the organizations with which they remained, but not both. In all cases, however, where connections were used by the organization stars, the connections were not of the intimate kind, that is, none of the organization stars came from wealthy or prominent families as evidenced by father's job status. This probably accounts for the fact that all except the professionals had to work their way up from low- to high-status positions. The well-connected, on the other hand, possessed both the intimate connections and exceptional educational qualifications.

The Restricted Movers

The importance of the strength of connections for ultimate success in the Iranian labor market is evidenced by another group of well-educated Iranians whose attributes place them between the organization stars and the well-connected—the restricted movers.

This group possessed advanced foreign educational degrees that had been privately funded. However, they did not have the same kinds of connections as the well-connected, who were associated with families influential in either the private manufacturing or public sector. Rather, their fathers came from the established upper-middle-class professional group—doctors, lawyers, and so on.

---

*For example, one respondent shifted from being supplies manager in NIOC, where he had charge of NIOC port facilities, to being supplies manager in a large private firm. "Coincidentally," this private firm often had access to NIOC's port facilities and thereby was able to bypass many of the delay problems encountered by others using southern ports.

In other words, these restricted movers had the wealth to obtain their education but not the direct contacts in the expanding modern sector.

As such, these well-educated Iranians, whose degrees trained them for specialization in growing areas such as systems and engineering or production, were coveted by private sector employers to fill middle management positions related to the maintenance of some aspect of the imported technology. But they were not organization members in good enough standing to aspire to the higher managerial positions reserved for a closed circle of trusted associates. In order for this to be the general case, Iranian employers would have had to be more willing to accept professional management divorced from the founders of the firm. As noted in Chapter 4, only one organization was considering this possibility.

In addition, the technical jobs accorded the restricted movers often entailed a level of working experience well beyond that held by these new graduates. The jobs therefore overutilized capabilities and tended to frustrate the jobholder. Thus, on the one hand, their education helped to find them a high-level job but, on the other hand, made them victims of the employers' credentialism, which sees, in this manpower-short economy, education as the ultimate substitute for experience.

The best advantage the well-educated professionals in the modern industrial sector had was in their attractiveness to other organizations in the industry that were willing to bargain on an individual basis for their services.* This, coupled with no defined promotional paths and low job satisfaction in the present organization, engendered raiding and voluntary job quits. Ultimately, the well-educated Iranian would change organizations many times before settling in one firm where his position, though very well paid, remained relatively static and comparable to his initial starting position.

The organizational stars, the well-connected, and the restricted movers include what Bill defines as three ideal types: the technocrat, the maneuverer, and the follower.

> The Technocrats are primarily concerned with carrying out the particular tasks for which they have been trained. They are intent on modifying and repairing the existing system [but not of fostering fundamental change] in order that they might go on with their various activities. As such, the Technocrats are alienated on grounds of procedure, and include administrators, managers, and many professional people.

---

*This degree of mobility naturally only applied to the well-educated professionals in more diverse industries. Professionals at NIOC, for example, had difficulty in moving within Iran because their skills were so specific to the oil industry and the industry was government-controlled.

> The Maneuverers are the defenders of the traditional power network. They are the manipulators. . . . Their modern education and formal skills are reserve power handles since they understand the traditional web best . . . because of personal ties they know that they can always maneuver into better positions.
>
> The Followers are those individuals who float in the safest and smoothest direction. They are the trailers of power who gravitate toward the strongest personalities, groups, and classes.[15]

Because precise identification of these three groups necessitates an in-depth knowledge of a person's personality, division of the sample according to these categories is not possible. As a general statement, however, the followers and the maneuverers are thought to outnumber the technocrats considerably.

Missing from any part of the discussion so far are what Bill calls the uprooters, and what Zonis calls the elite. The former are educated, middle-class, political dissidents found in groups such as writers, artists, professors, and students. The elite are upper class and in many respects are just very successful maneuverers. They are well connected, well educated, well traveled, and play prominent parts in the government either in primary or secondary roles. Some of the well-connected were destined to become part of this group.

A good example of uprooters can be found in an article in the *Washington Post* about 11 Iranians convicted of subversive activities. The article reads: "Eleven Iranian 'terrorists' convicted of Communist affiliation last month began a series of personal pleas for leniency before a military appeals court today. . . . All of the accused *have foreign university degrees* and were sentenced April 12 after what critics called a 'show trial' to prison terms ranging from life to three years. . . . None of the defendants was charged with any actual terrorist action in Iran."[16] Their education places them in different categories from the peasant revolutionaries. As the article indicated, their activities were inclined to be more verbal than physical.

The inevitable conclusion of both quantitative and qualitative analyses of career success is that those without foreign university degrees but, most importantly, without good connections, suffered almost insurmountable disadvantages. This group of Iranian-educated make up the remainder of the restricted movers.

To an Iranian employer in the private sector, there are two major problems to be handled in regard to HLM. First, all the highest level administrative and financial tasks must be assigned to a closed circle of trusted associates. The tasks can be subdivided in accordance with manpower availability. Second, technically knowledgeable individuals must be found to set up and maintain the imported technology. In this instance, family members are preferable as well, but foreign-trained professionals with technical or specialized education are acceptable.

But, although Iranian employers had shown a willingness to grant responsibility to those with foreign technical education, the bias had not been extended to include Iranians with Iranian technical degrees. As a result, without connections or the other advantages of the organization stars, the Iranian-educated, regardless of field of specialization, was confined to the low-status administrative posts of chiefs and assistant chiefs.* At best, this kind of restricted mover faced a number of lateral intraorganizational job shifts. Interorganizationally, mobility was severely limited because of their poor bargaining position in the outside market. They might aptly be termed as the true disadvantaged of the middle class.

FINANCIAL OPPORTUNITIES: PRIVATE AND GOVERNMENT SECTORS

Restricted social mobility for the majority of Iranians in HLM categories was but one outcome of the organizational practices in Iran. Financial opportunities for many were also limited. In the public sector, for example, civil servants in high-status administrative positions had opportunities to supplement their government salaries through multiple jobholdings that were not open to the lower-level administrators. In addition, salary data from all organization studies underscore that remuneration between different job levels and within the same job levels were subject to large inequities.

Multiple Jobholding

Multiple jobholding was often a significant aspect of an individual's career pattern in Iran. The incidence of second jobs was also mostly commonly associated with high-status HLM positions. For example, Marvin Zonis reported that only 20 percent of his sample of Iranian elite did *not* hold other jobs.[17] In this study of HLM, roughly 24 percent of the respondents stated that they had a second job. But 42 percent of those in the higher positions of department heads or above worked at a second job compared to only 16 percent of those in the lower status HLM positions. This relationship between job status and multiple jobholding became more striking when sector affiliation was considered. Of those in high positions in the government, 75 percent held another job, whereas only 27 percent of the highly placed individuals in the private sector also did so.

---

*Note the difference between the organization stars and this group of restricted movers. The former entered the organizations with which they remained in the 1960s; most were new labor market entrants at this time. The latter group entered the organizations at a later date, although their first jobs may have been with other organizations during the 1960s in similar low-status positions.

The multiple jobholder, regardless of sector affiliation, spent approximately 11 hours per week at the second job. The work hours in the primary job did not vary significantly from those of others in the organization. This information on hours appears to suggest that the time burden imposed by other jobs was not severe. However, there is reason to suspect that the hours data were not highly accurate. All respondents tended to report hours of work in their primary job as being the standard work week and did not or would not comment upon the actual amount worked. Exceptions were those who regularly worked overtime. Moreover, most respondents who stated that they held second jobs could not accurately say how many hours they worked in the other jobs per week. The time spent varied greatly from week to week. This suggests that there were times when the second job did indeed distract the respondent from the primary job duties.

Within the private sector, there was an income motivation for holding a second job among those in the low-status job group. Those with second jobs in low positions in this sector earned on the average $308 per month less than their organizational counterparts who did not hold other jobs. At the high-status job positions, however, the difference in income was insignificant. Moreover, monthly earnings from the second job were around $132 less for those in high-status positions than for those in low-status positions.

This suggests that highly placed individuals in the private sector held other jobs for reasons that were unrelated to income. Their second jobs increased their self-esteem or utilized energies that were not fully developed on the main job. (See below for descriptions of second job occupations.) Second job income was only 18 percent of the total monthly income. For low-status jobholders, on the other hand, the second job made up 44 percent of their monthly income.

Within the public sector, multiple jobholding occurred partly in response to the desire for more income. Public sector salaries were far below those of the private sector (see below). Earnings from the second job were about 30 percent of total monthly income for high-status jobholders and roughly 40 percent of total monthly income for low-status jobholders.

In contrast to the private sector, public sector employees who held other jobs earned significantly more than their counterparts who did not hold other jobs. For both low- and high-status jobholders, monthly income in the main job was about 25 to 50 percent more per month, on the average, than for those without other jobs. The fact that multiple jobholding in the public sector was associated with the higher income brackets reinforces the idea that ability to hold other jobs in the public sector came with increased status and tenure within the organization. (Government salaries are also related to tenure.) Those with less standing in the organization, as evidenced by lower incomes, seemed to be less able to obtain second jobs. Most certainly the income incentive to hold other jobs was just as vital, if not more so.

Examination of the types of second jobs that were held helps to clarify some of the above relationships. Public servants who moonlighted tended to work in their second jobs almost exclusively for the government, either directly or indirectly as private consultants offering engineering, managerial, or computer-related services or as entrepreneurs selling imported products to government organizations. In contrast, the second occupation of those whose main job was in the private sector tended to be less professionally oriented or less related to activities or organizations associated with the main job. For example, many moonlighted as landlords, gentlemen farmers, or professors.

The fact that most of the multiple jobholders from the government held second jobs that were professionally oriented and within the government service confirms earlier comments; that is, higher salaries are associated with multiple jobholding because they indicate increased ability to moonlight. Indeed, the possibility of obtaining government contracts as a private consultant or entrepreneur is greater for someone who has been working in the civil service long enough and in a position high enough to make useful contacts within the government.

This moonlighting for the government also served to enhance one's status, or power position, within the political organization and, additionally, decreased the opportunites for other similarly qualified or educated individuals to gain entrance into the government hierarchy. In short, the assignment of government contracts to established civil servants was a means by which the public sector could distribute the greatest number of tasks among a favored group of persons in much the same way as the private sector divided top administrative duties among the available supply of trusted relatives and friends.[18]

Reward Patterns in the Main Job

The evidence collected from the sample of Iranian HLM does show that individual characteristics carry much more weight than actual job duties per-formed. Holding level of education and job status constant, the foreign-educated earned a salary premium of around 14 to 30 percent more than the Iranian-educated. In addition, foreigners received approximately an extra 10 percent in salary.

With respect to differences in education, some salary differentials can be justified on the basis that foreign-trained personnel do not need as much prelim-inary supervision to perform job duties, particularly for duties relating to the technical aspects of the production method, and therefore should be paid more initially. However, the differential between foreign and Iranian educational back-grounds persisted even among the most experienced personnel.

Most important, significant differences were as well noted when the relationship between salary and recruitment method was examined. Those hired by friends or relatives received 5 to 25 percent more than those hired into similar positions by other means, for example, in direct response to newspaper ads. This positive relationship between salary and recruitment by friends and relatives is an important finding. The method of recruitment as obtained through answers to interview questions (which did not accurately assess the relative status or power position of the friends and relatives) did not have a noticeable impact upon the job status into which one was initially hired, but it is interesting to note that it did often entail a considerable difference in salary.*

Notable variations were also found between private and government sector jobs. As was anticipated by the discussion in the previous chapter, the private sector tended to reward the least tenured staff members (those with the organization one year or less) 5 to 19 percent more than individuals in similar positions who had been with the organization three years or more. In the government sector, however, the long-tenured organization members were paid considerably more than the new entrants. Persons with more than three years' tenure received, in fact, about 60 percent more salary than new organizational entrants in equal positions.

The average private sector salary for high-status administrative posts falling within the range of this study was between $2,000 and $5,000 per month; for the low-status positions the range was between $800 and $1,500 per month. (Seventy rials in 1976, the time of the study, was equal to $1 U.S.) In the government sector, salaries were 30 to 100 percent less than those in the private sector. High-status positions received, on the average, between $1,600 and $3,000 per month; low-status positions were rewarded with $400 to $800 per month.

The discrepancy between low-status and high-status position salaries, it should also be noted, was greatest in the government. High-status jobholders in the government received about four times as much as low-status jobholders in the same organization. In the private sector, scales were more closely related. The bottom of the high-status scale was only twice that of the bottom of the low status.†

---

*The question in the interview schedule that read "How did you learn about this job?" did not capture the relative importance of the respondents' connections and also did not give information on whether the connections with friends and relatives were within or outside the firms. As a result, the responses could not indicate to any degree how connections may have influenced hiring position.

†It should be noted that in the private sector the pay differentials between low-status administrative jobs and blue-collar positions were equally as large. But this was not the case between the low-status administrative jobs and servant categories in the government. A long-tenured servant in the government could earn equivalent salary to a new entrant at the low administrative positions. Thus there was a bunching of salary scales at all but the high-status levels.

The differences between low- and high-status remuneration in the government were even larger when it is considered that the high-status jobholders also had greater opportunities to earn additional income from a second job. In both sectors, however, inequities in the low-status job scales were larger. Personal attributes, such as being hired by friends and relatives, merited a much higher salary increase over others in the same position among the low-status jobholders than among high-status jobholders.

Benefits in the form of living allowances, productivity bonuses as required by law, and merit bonuses could also be as much as 60 percent of an organizational member's salary. All the salary relationships described above held true when total average monthly income (salary plus monetary benefits) was used in place of average monthly salary. This means that the rewarding of benefits was proportionate to salary levels.

CONCLUSIONS

In brief, findings in the chapter showed that family influences in Iran affected career success in a radically different way than in the United States. In the United States, the greatest impact of the family is felt at the educational level before a career is begun. In Iran, on the other hand, family connections most influence career success after education is completed and when entry is made into the labor market. In short, connections are more relevant to career success than any other factor.

The analysis of career profiles verified these findings. The outer fringe Iranian minorities, for example, who did have good educational degrees, did not generally prosper until they used their connections in ethnic communities. The organization stars were able to compensate for either poor connections or impractical educational backgrounds through long tenure in an organization, which helped them to receive subsidized education, in the case of the government, or valuable job experience and most particularly intimate connections with the organization's most influential members, in the case of the private sector.

The formation of connections in the government sector was the most auspicious factor, as persons of similar job experience and education, but without the patronage, were not given the same promotional opportunities. In the private sector, tenure began when organizations were expanding in the 1960s. Thus individuals were then able to receive a wider range of pertinent job experiences and more contact with top organizational members than was permitted to organizational members entering the organization in low-status positions in the 1970s. The well-connected achieved immediate career success with the promise of additional opportunities because of influential connections and foreign education.

For organizational members who first entered organizations in the 1970s, regardless of earlier job experiences in other organizations, increase in job status was limited without the proper connections. Members in this group have been called the restricted movers. For the Iranian-educated, career prospects were confined to the lowest managerial levels. For the foreign-educated, entrance into the administrative hierarchy was higher, but movement into top positions was open only to the closest friends and relatives.

The kindship-oriented organizational practices produced negative behavior within the HLM labor market. In general, mobility between organizations and among jobs within the same organization can be beneficial and healthy for the operation of the labor market. However, in the Iranian context, mobility did not perform such a role. For those at the bottom of the job status scale, mobility was a fruitless endeavor as job experience went unrewarded. Expertise developed in one job did not qualify as promotion material. Many of these persons were underutilized and overeducated in these jobs.

At the other extreme, the well-educated restricted movers were very mobile organizationally. But their mobility was equally unproductive. It was motivated by job frustrations resulting from overutilization in their jobs and better salary levels than could be had by moving. They did not remain with one organization long enough to develop their skills fully. Thus, whereas a lack of organizational mobility is usually a sign of lack of opportunity, a high degree of organizational mobility is a sign of opportunity being used to compensate for frustrating job experiences within the organization.

The confinement of a large number of Iranian university graduates in positions that do not necessarily require such education, and the high premiums paid to foreign-educated personnel independently of job experience, point to excessive credentialism in the labor market and the poor trade-offs permitted between education and experience. This is one of the ironies of the operation of the labor market in Iran. Despite the shortage of manpower, employers had done little to adapt to the situation. In part, their inactivity was fostered by the short-age of manpower who could help train others and the high turnover thresholds that discouraged investment in employee-subsidized training. But it was also a function of managerial inexperience.

The high incidence of multiple jobholding among government employees, particularly high-status jobholders, was also an adjustment mechanism that compensated for low income levels and malutilization on the main job. By per-mitting the employees to become involved professionally with other projects with the government, the public sector organizations not only undermined the quality of time spent on the main job but limited job opportunities for others.

In the private sector, the amount of multiple jobholding was not as great. Moreover, second jobs of private sector employees were less likely to conflict with main job duties because they were not as professionally oriented. One reason for this difference perhaps was the attitudes of the private sector employers, who were less willing to tolerate multiple jobholding than were public administrators.

Salary inequities served to demoralize further many HLM participants. The net result was a system that valued and rewarded personal qualities and relationships and minimized job performance.

NOTES

1. The Farsi version of the interview schedule is contained in an appendix to Gail Cook Johnson, "Institutional Processes Governing the Behavior of High-Level Manpower in Iran," Ph.D. dissertation, Massachusetts Institute of Technology, 1978. Due to the fact that an employer would not always permit the author and the trained interviewers the time to interview employers, the schedule was also devised so that self-response was possible. Thirty-eight responses were by this method. Self-administered responses did not appear to be different from those that were obtained through interviewing, although a greater occurrence of no responses to some variables was noted in these instances. For an analysis of no responses and details on the interview process, see ibid.

2. James A. Bill, "Class Analysis and the Dialectics of Modernization in the Middle East," *International Journal of Middle East Studies* 3 (1972): 425. Bill, *The Politics of Iran: Groups, Classes and Modernization* (Columbus, Ohio: Merrill, 1972), uses the power relationship as a basis for his specific discussion on Iran's social structure. R. W. Gable, "Culture and Administration in Iran," *Middle East Journal* 13 (1959): 408–09, also relates how the social system is based upon the division of labor.

3. For a discussion of this aspect, see James A. Bill, "The Plasticity of Informal Politics: The Case of Iran," paper delivered at the Conference on the Structure of Power in Islamic Iran, University of California, Los Angeles, June 1969; Leonard Binder, *Iran: Political Development in a Changing Society* (Berkeley and Los Angeles: University of California Press, 1962); and Andrew F. Westwood, "Politics of Distrust in Iran," *Annals of the American Academy of Political and Social Sciences*, no. 358, March 1965, pp. 397–415.

4. See Johnson, op. cit., for a more detailed discussion of the job status measurement.

5. For detailed distributions on primary characteristics of respondents and their fathers, see ibid., Appendix E.

6. Peter M. Blau and Otis D. Duncan, *The American Occupational Structure* (New York: Wiley, 1967).

7. For a discussion of path analysis, see ibid.; and N. H. Nie et al., *Statistical Package for the Social Sciences*, 2nd ed. (New York: McGraw-Hill, 1975).

8. For a detailed discussion of hypotheses behind the model, see Johnson, op. cit.

9. See ibid. for discussion of such results.

10. Bill, *Politics of Iran*, p. 69.

11. Ibid., p. 68.

12. The exact numbers of Iranians subsidized by the government to study abroad is unknown. The Pahlavi Foundation, according to Robert Graham, *Iran: The Illusion of Power* (New York: St. Martin's Press, 1978), p. 156, had financed the education abroad of 12,000 students since its inception to March 1977. Some of this was loan assistance, but only about 25 percent of the total sum was reimbursable. Financing for education abroad also came directly from various government departments.

13. In Zonis' terms, minorities under the Shah's regime were accepted as "boarders" who were accommodated as long as they agreed with the majority claims. See Marvin Zonis, *The Political Elite of Iran* (Princeton, N.J.: Princeton University Press, 1976), pp. 274–76.

14. Bill, *Politics of Iran*, pp. 55–56.

15. Ibid., p. 72.

16. William Branigan, "Terrorists Appeal Tehran Sentences," *Washington Post*, May 11, 1977, sec. A, p. 12 [emphasis authors].

17. Zonis, op. cit., p. 189.

18. Ibid., pp. 189–91, notices the same kind of government behavior directed toward the elite.

6

CONFLICT TO CRISIS

Economic history suggests that, in the long-run, industrialization leads to large, efficient organizations managed on behalf of shareholders by a battalion of skilled technocrats.[1] Such a prospect dictates that, whatever the cultural peculiarities of a nation, some advanced form of meritocracy must exist if a country is to become highly industrialized.[2] This means that at each stage of development, institutional arrangements must be brought in balance with the new demands of economic expansion.

One conventional view of the development process holds that the required institutional and social adjustments will be forthcoming under the pressures of rapid economic growth. The analysis presented here, however, does not support this supposition. Under the pressures of rapid industrialization in Iran, chronic imbalances were aggravated. Indeed, what was so striking about Iran under the Shah was that ambitious modernization plans were attempted with little change in the elitist social order. As a consequence of the barriers in the labor market, HLM, as well as the traditional working class, were subject to the frustrations of limited upward mobility and little prospect for economic improvement. The continued backwardness of both public and private sector institutions resulted in the failure of industrialization because it did not integrate the emerging educated middle and working classes.

A REVIEW

The oil wealth of Iran offered economic opportunities rarely envisioned by other developing countries. Not wanting to take the slower course of economic growth given by labor-intensive industry, and presented with a home demand for consumer products as a result of the new revenue in the country, industrial expansion was guided toward developing, first, the very capital-intensive oil industry and, second, industries specializing in the manufacture of consumer durables. The strategy of rapid industrialization led to growing dependence on foreign technology and expertise and exaggerated income inequality and created unbalanced growth.

This particular development pattern confronted formidable problems. If indeed "the proportion of the work force engaged in agriculture is a rough index of the degree of industrialization of a society,"[3] Iran's stage of development was not advanced. In 1969, 50 percent of the labor force was employed in agriculture.[4] The infrastructure necessary to support modern industry was lacking. Moreover, the commitment to technology and the shortage of Iranian HLM, which tied the Iranian development effort to foreign expertise, was repugnant to the country's growing nationalism. Unless Iranian manpower was significantly upgraded, continued foreign presence was essential if Iran was not only to maintain, but also expand and improve, the capital base. The goals of development therefore included a major expansion of the industrial base and infrastructure and, concomitantly, a massive increase in the skill level of the Iranian population. The kind of leadership offered to oversee the modernization effort and its recognition of the obstacles to industrialization was embedded in the economic and social structures of the country were therefore of crucial importance. In this regard, this analysis has been able to offer significant insight into why the development strategy failed.

The leadership of the society was centered around the Shah and his regime. With the monarch as its head, Iran had a carefully constructed set of pecking orders, or classes. Below the Shah came his family, his ministers, the top civil servants and the leaders of the private sector enterprises, the middle-class bureaucrats, and the peasants in descending order. In the upper echelons, a person could carry dual roles and cross class boundaries, but rank and proximity to the Shah governed one's ultimate benefits and lifestyle.

The monarchy was preserved by the selective application of rewards or economic and physical sanctions directed personally by the Shah through his control of the civil service, intelligence and military agencies, and ownership in private sector industrial enterprises. This pervasive influence of the head of government served to divide, and thereby control, the various substrata of society. Any effective leadership for the development effort therefore could only be expected from the Shah himself.

The Shah was not only desirous of increasing Iran's stature in the world but was also faced with the necessity of appeasing the demands of the various social groups in his country and of ensuring the supremacy of its armed forces. As a result, he directed that the oil revenues be spent upon a too diverse an array of projects. Necessary investments in Iranian infrastructure and education were diluted by expenditures on ventures abroad, subsidies to a variety of unconnected industrial projects within Iran, the establishment of numerous welfare programs, and heavy outlays in the military sphere. When the development goals were devised in 1974, it was mistakenly assumed that oil revenues would be available in increasing amounts to support this diversification. Throughout the period massive import leakages and the flight of capital abroad left the country excessively dependent upon oil income.

These oil revenues dropped sharply with the undercutting of oil prices by other OPEC members and meant that the government, by 1977, had to accept a slower rate of growth. It was then faced with the impossible task of convincing a skeptical populace that it must now lower previously heightened expectations. In short, development plans were very unbalanced and were thereby doomed for failure. Coupled with the reaction to repressive government policy, unbalanced growth spawned social rather than industrial revolution. The inability of the majority of the population to participate in the political system and the lack of broadening of economic incentives left the established order vulnerable to instability.

This was aptly illustrated by the constraints placed upon management in the various institutions of the society. Within the private sector, for example, the ad hoc nature of government policy, which permitted laws to be suddenly repealed or enacted without prior notification, fostered such strong feelings of insecurity about the future that entrepreneurs (the owner-managers of this study) were only willing to commit themselves to short-run risk taking and quick profit. Fear of reprisals for independent action also prevented any one entrepreneur from initiating and encouraging effective group action among industrialists. The lack of collective effort meant that the private sector could not properly challenge the public sector's monopolization of scarce resources relating to both physical infrastructures and to HLM or to influence the specifics of government policy.

Under such a system, it was not surprising that the industrialists replicated in their organizations the management style of the Shah. Seeking to maintain their status within society, the industrialists built their empires around family members or close family friends for maximum centralized control. This was the basis of the extended kinship system. Defying the demand of efficiency for their rapidly expanding organizations, enterprises developed along functional rather than divisional lines to ensure further the control of the company elite. Authority did not extend down the line for even the most insignificant operating decisions; nor did channels of two-way communication develop among hierarchical levels except at the very top.

The subordination of long-run economic efficiency to immediate self-interest hampered the attainment of goals set for the course of development at the private sector level. The acute shortage of HLM already generated by economic growth was aggravated by industrialists who preferred their top Iranian personnel to be close kin and ideally educated abroad.

In the organizations studied, operations expanded vertically in response to market imperfections. The vertical integration, in addition, was being led by foreign licensors. With the exception of the foreign-managed firm, no part of the technology was adapted to suit better the skills of the indigenous population. This course of organizational development therefore committed Iranian industrialists to inefficient economies of scale. With respect to manpower needs, foreign technologies made obsolete the skills of Iranian-educated university graduates.

Within the public service sector, technological constraints were not at question. But the active intervention of the Shah in the decision-making processes of the civil service prevented the development of efficient organizational structures. Intent upon maintaining their power positions, top civil servants assigned persons to positions on the basis of their connections.

The most tragic consequences of the inefficiencies, that is, the waste of human resources, are verified by the analysis of individual career paths. Family background, admittedly, has implications for one's career regardless of country. But the influence of the family in Iran was shown to be particularly extensive. In contrast to the United States, family status not only helped to predict the quality of one's education (foreign versus Iranian) but, most significantly, influenced initial, and hence subsequent, job placements. Among the vast majority of HLM who were educated in Iran, career opportunities were limited to the lowest managerial positions. In these positions, they were underutilized.

While the Iranian-educated had pertinent reasons for feeling disillusioned with their lot in the labor market, so also did the better-educated groups. At best, the foreign-educated Iranians were left to follow career paths that stopped short of the most rewarding positions unless they were well-connected or could find a niche with the outer fringe ethnic community.

Moreover, despite the fact that most of these foreign-educated restricted movers were well qualified, in a formal sense, they lacked on-the-job training and guidance. This produced a high level of frustration and discouraged organizational loyalty. Better opportunities were always perceived to lie elsewhere. Among top-level civil servants who were tied to government service in some capacity such as pensions and long-term loans, low income levels and dissatisfaction with the main job were compensated for by multiple jobholding. Both multiple jobholding and brief job tenure were counterproductive to organizational development.

In summary, the leadership offered by the Shah for the development effort exacerbated rather than curbed inefficiencies of institutional processes at work in the labor market. Due to uncertainty, often created by the government, firms failed to invest in manpower or research and development, thereby creating uninspiring work environments and repressive hierarchies. This process of stagnation was further reinforced by the response of labor. Facing relatively flat career paths, employees accommodated to malutilization, reflected in high turnover rates and multiple jobholding. The three key groups of government, employers, and manpower were caught in a situation of negative reinforcement that undermined the formation of unified commitment to the development goals of the nation and encouraged the disintegration of the industrial order.

TRADITIONALISM

This overview of Iranian organizations also reflects the experiences of other developing countries. Economic backwardness in South American nations, for example, has been attributed to kinship orientations that restrict upward mobility, create a general atmosphere of mistrust, foster a lack of commitment to long-term goals, and so on.[5] In short, "family centeredness has been typical of early industrialization everywhere."[6]

The extended kinship system is such a universal barrier to development because it is a manifestation of underlying cultural values that are common to traditional societies. Specifically, adherence to traditional values (or traditionalism) means that a person's social relationship with another is judged to be more important than objective standards of performance. In the developed countries, on the other hand, value judgments are more inclined to rest upon some universal standards that are applied to a person's actual achievements.[7] The traditional values are, of course, antagonistic to the development of a strong, and large, manpower base skilled to undertake and lead the development process in the absence of very detailed directives and supervision from above.

The lack of any kind of standard system to appraise performance and the absence of promotional opportunities for most individuals, which were noted in the organizations studied, are manifestations of traditional cultural values in Iran. The persistence of traditional values among the Iranian elite was in part encouraged by the instability created by such economic circumstances as high inflation, high interest rates, and manpower shortages and the need for political survival within the elitist culture.

The inevitable conclusion to be reached is that, in conjunction with economic planning, efforts must be made to move the society toward an achievement-oriented institutions if economic stability is to be assured.[8] The Shah's universalization of the higher education system through the institution of university entrance examinations was such an attempt to bring the society toward a meritocracy. However, the policy did not carry through to the labor market in an effective manner.

Such laws as the share participation laws and the labor legislation were designed to give industrial workers greater financial gains, but fell short of providing for their greatest needs, that of greater self-esteem and increasing job status. In addition, these policies affected only a small proportion of the labor force, particularly neglecting agricultural workers and employees within establishments of less than ten persons. Iranians doubted the laws' sincerity and assessed them only in terms of their political merit—with disastrous effects. Iranian university students, for example, receiving as they did education unsuited to the demands of both private and public institutions, became a frustrated and politically motivated group set against the Shah's regime.

The need to develop an achievement-oriented society does not mean that developing countries must pattern themselves exactly on the more economically advanced nations. Comparison between organizational structures and management styles of the developed countries suggests that there is more than one way to be effective. In Japan, for example, organizations have been structured around the family concept. The management function is most heavily distributed among middle management and promotion and job placement are functions of seniority and education. In contrast, German organizations are highly centralized, with the bulk of decision-making authority concentrated at the top; promotional opportunities are specified by functional area.[9] These differing experiences demonstrate that "achievement [-oriented] values [can] seemingly [emerge] out of a redefinition of traditional values, rather than the adoption of new ones."[10]

CHANGE THROUGH ECONOMIC DEVELOPMENT

The redefinition of values may, of course, begin through the process of development itself. The oldest Iranian-managed firm in this study demonstrated this impact. This establishment contrasted with the other Iranian firms in that it had developed a more achievement-oriented personnel system that permitted a few professional managers to penetrate, after long service, the upper echelons of the family managerial elite. The evolution of the firm to this stage was attributed to its age and consequently to the dying out of the founding entrepreneur and his family. Conceivably, therefore, further disappearance of the original entrepreneurs can propel the creation of stable and well-run organizations designed to utilize human resources.

However, this process of change is too slow in comparison to the rapid pace of industrialization that was set by Iran's development plans. The majority of Iranian industrial organizations are either government-controlled or young, private firms operated by foreigners and/or Iranians. The government firms that in the past served as examples for the new private firms showed no signs of change and were very much dependent upon foreign involvement and political support (for example, the National Iranian Oil Company). The young firms were far from reaching the stage of maturation accomplished by the oldest firm in the sample. Furthermore, the continued dominance of foreign management in some establishments retarded the maturing process. As was demonstrated by one of the firms that was examined, the occupation of top positions by a foreign elite prevented the advancement of the native-born population regardless of the degree of formalization at the lower levels of the organization.

FUTURE PROSPECTS

How adept will the new Islamic republic that is presently taking shape in Iran be in avoiding the pitfalls of unbalanced growth? The revolution in Iran has brought with it expectations for both greater political participation and more equitable economic development. However, the legacy of underdeveloped institutions, further undermined by a year of turmoil, indicates that fulfilling these expectations may be beyond the capacity of the current regime.

At the macro level, many critical factors threaten economic growth. The new government has inherited the foreign technology that was installed during the Shah's regime. Because sufficient numbers of Iranians were not upgraded and foreigners have left the country, the capacity to maintain or adapt technology does not exist.

This is of particular relevance to the oil industry. By April 1979, Iran was able to produce 4.7 million barrels of oil a day. Average production has been targeted between 3.5 to 4 million barrels per day. This level is only about 2 million below prerevolution standards. Such a high volume of production therefore appears encouraging. However, in the long run, foreign expertise will be needed to oversee maintainance operations and exploration. In addition, according to Western newspaper reports, political instability threatens the positions of those few Iranians with management expertise in the oil industry.[11] Without sustained oil revenues, the new regime will be unable to enact a comprehensive economic plan.

The continued dependence upon oil and a lack of diversification still leaves a narrow industrial base and prospects of instability in export earnings. Past emphasis upon import substitution in industry and the poor performance of the agricultural sector have left the country a large importer of agricultural goods. It will take a long time before this can be reversed.

Within the private sector, the future of large industrial organizations such as were studied here is not optimistic. Key infrastructure institutions that under the Shah were inadequate have been set back further by the revolution. Universities and transportation, for example, are in disarray.

In addition, while the new government will most likely consent eventually to the recruitment of foreign experts in the oil industry in order to ensure the main source of Iran's income, it is unlikely that it will be politically feasible to allow the same importation of foreign technology and expertise to mainstay the private industrial sector. Indeed, from the investment point of view, the revolution led to the loss of many local entrepreneurs and their capital when they fled the country. The government will be hard-pressed to entice Iranians into private entrepreneurship, let alone foreigners.

Given the limited support facilities and the decline in domestic demand that was fostered by the slowdown in economic growth, rapid expansion of the industrial sector is not feasible. Therefore the large profits that encouraged investment under the Shah are less likely to be an incentive. Uncertainty about what profit-making schemes and financial arrangements will be permitted under Islamic ideals endorsed by the government will also deter investors. In short, private sources of foreign capital and technology under these circumstances will not be forthcoming.

In the public domain, the public sector that played a leading, albeit often inefficient, role in development has virtually been destroyed and must be rebuilt before it can hope to confront economic issues. The dislocation of established government structures has created enormous social problems that will divert attention and resources from development initiatives.

Many of the social groups that supported the overthrow of the Shah did so more as a protest against the Shah than as a full endorsement of Islamic republican ideals. Ayatollah Khomeini had become a symbol for change around whom diverse social classes could rally and voice their dissent. The referendum held in early 1979 to determine the form of government cannot be construed as a mandate of popular support, given the limited choices that were offered and the election procedures that were used.* Resurgent ethnic and regional divisions that came into the open soon after the Shah was overthrown, particularly among the Kurdish population, serve to undermine both political and economic efforts to consolidate power.

At the level of individual institutions, this analysis has isolated key factors that retarded institution building. Economic performance under the new regime will depend upon a reversal of the patterns that characterized institutional behavior under the Shah. In this respect, the revolution has created some positive opportunities for beneficial organizational change. While most definitely problematic to the salvaging of the private sector, the removal of foreigners and the departure of many members of the past regime's elite at least now open avenues for Iranians to move to higher echelons in both the private and public sectors. The "new deal" in emotions[12] that can be offered by a new government may allow for an improved accommodation of labor unions, agricultural workers, the government, and management.

However, if the elite in the government and private sectors are appointed or achieve power due to close ties with the current regime, the promise of improved mobility and performance-based management may not arise. Fragmenta-

---

*Ballots were red or green, one signifying a vote for an Islamic republic and the other for the maintenance of the monarchy. The voter's name and address had to be specified on the ballot. The election results were announced prior to completion of ballot counting.

tion along ethnic and regional lines may add to the polarization of institutions and continue to exclude Iranians on the basis of factors other than economic suitability.

The revolution, in addition, cannot have done away with the pervasive feelings of mistrust and cynicism that were generated under the previous regime. These sentiments do not encourage the change in values or the new deal in emotions that would be necessary if the new government is to act as a catalyst to more open and responsive institutions.

Already the new regime has met with opposition from the National Front with the resignation of its leader, Karim Sanjabi, as foreign minister and from the more violent reactions of the political left. These groups have protested the "despotic" methods and secret dealings of the Revolutionary Council and its Islamic revolutionary committees, known as Komitehs, and have questioned the qualifications and identities of council members.* White-collar workers, as well as laborers and students, have been among the protesters.[13] Such criticism, particularly as it was preceded by the attempted resignation of the government's prime minister, Mehdi Bazargan, suggests that there is a retreat to methods practiced by the Shah.

Economic development therefore may be severely retarded because political structures and incentives are not conducive to the evolution of modern economic institutions. A punitive atmosphere and uncertainty engendered by political instability create a system prone to polarization and regression to traditionalism. The failure of industrialization under the Shah to integrate the various sectors of the society resulted in the disintegration of the ruling dictatorship. Without efforts directed toward institutional reform to unite the classes of the society with common goals, the emotions invoked by the revolution will not be put to rest.

NOTES

1. See, for example, Charles Kindelberger, *Economic Growth in France and Britain, 1850-1950* (Cambridge, Mass.: Harvard University Press, 1964); and John K. Galbraith, *The New Industrial State* (Boston: Houghton Mifflin, 1967).

2. This is the "logic of industrialization" presented by Clark Kerr, John T. Dunlop, Frederick Harbison, and Charles A. Myers, *Industrialism and Industrial Man* (Cambridge, Mass.: Harvard University Press, 1960).

---

*Ibrahim Yazdi, former deputy prime minister for revolutionary affairs and now foreign minister and confidant of Ayatollah Khomeini since the latter's stay in France, has been under particular attack. When Sanjabi resigned his post, he stated that the foreign ministry was being undermined by Shahriar Rouhani, the acting ambassador to the United States and Yazdi's son-in-law, who was taking instructions from the Central Komiteh rather than the foreign ministry.

3. Ibid., p. 39.

4. The 1969 figure is an average of statistics obtained from the biannual survey of the Ministry of Labor and Social Affairs, *Household Sample Survey, May-June 1969* and *December 1969-January 1970.* The spring figure places agricultural employment at 53 percent, while the latter survey gives a figure of 47 percent.

5. See, for example, articles in Seymour Martin Lipset and Aldo Solari, eds., *Elites in Latin America* (New York: Oxford University Press, 1969); and Harry M. Makler, "Labor Problems of Native, Migrant and Foreign-Born Members of the Recife Industrial Elite," *Journal of Developing Areas*, October 1974; and Albert Lauterback, *Enterprises in Latin America* (Ithaca, N.Y.: Cornell University Press, 1966).

6. W. Paul Strassman, "The Industrialist," in *Continuity in Latin America* ed. John J. Johnson (Palo Alto: Calif.: Stanford University Press, 1978), p. 169.

7. Talcott Parsons, *The Social System* (Glencoe, Ill.: Free Press, 1951); and "Pattern Variables Revisited," *American Sociological Review* 25 (1960): 464-83., developed two kinds of pattern variables to refer to values in developing and developed nations, respectively. These are the ascriptive-particularistic mode, where individuals are judged in terms of inherited attributes (ascription) and valued in terms of personal relationships rather than by objective standards (particularism); and the achievement-universalistic pattern, where persons are judged by performance (achievement) and organizations operate by objective standards (universalism).

8. This conclusion was also reached by Raymond D. Gastil, "Middle Class Impediments to Iranian Modernization," *Public Opinion Quarterly* 22 (1958): 325-39.

9. For a discussion of different management styles, see John L. Tarrant, "Worldwide Variations in Management Style," *Management Review*, April 1976, pp. 36-39.

10. Seymour Martin Lipset, "Values, Education and Entrepreneurship," in Lipset and Solari, op. cit., p. 35.

11. See Youssef M. Ibrahim, "Iran Lifts Oil Price 13% Beyond OPEC's," *New York Times*, April 16, 1979, pp. A1 and D2.

12. Alexander Gerschenkron, *Economic Backwardness in Historical Perspective* (Cambridge, Mass.: Harvard University Press, 1962), p. 25, wrote: "In a backward country, the great and sudden industrialization efforts call for a New Deal in emotions."

13. *New York Times*, April 18, 1979, p. A-1.

APPENDIX

EMPLOYEE INTERVIEW SCHEDULE

HIGH-LEVEL MANPOWER SURVEY

SECTION I: GENERAL INFORMATION

1. NAME: _____ 2. AGE: _____

3. SEX: male _____   4. NATIONALITY: _____

      female _____

5. MARITAL STATUS: single   ☐   married   ☐   divorced   ☐

                           separated ☐   widowed   ☐

6. NUMBER OF DEPENDENTS: _____

SECTION II: EDUCATIONAL BACKGROUND

7. Please specify the number of years that you have completed of university education:
_____years.

8. Please list below all the educational qualifications which you have been awarded, or for which you are currently studying, in the order of your most recent qualification to first:

QUALIFICATION (degree or certificate)	MAJOR FIELD OF STUDY, e.g. chemistry; law	DATE RECEIVED OR EXPECTED	NAME OF INSTITUTE OR SCHOOL	COUNTRY WHERE INSTITUTE OR SCHOOL IS LOCATED

9. If you have had any work-related training which did not offer an educational degree, please describe your type of training by checking the most appropriate category or categories below. If you have received more than one type, identify the one which has been most valuable for your present job by circling the appropriate letter:

    (a) Formal employer training programme (including regularly scheduled classes . . . .☐

    (b) On-the-job training without classes . . . .☐

    (c) Employer-sponsored scholarships (non-degree course) . . . .☐

    (d) Other: specify _____ . . . .☐

10. What were the actual number of months spent in obtaining the training you specified above as being most valuable? _____ months.

11. What speciality did you follow in the training you identified as being most valuable? (e.g. management training; accountancy; etc.)

          Speciality _____

SECTION III: CAREER HISTORY

In this section, you are asked about your present job and certain jobs that you have held in the past.

NOTE: If you are not an Iranian citizen, answer questions only with reference to jobs held in Iran. Iranian citizens should answer all questions fully, including reference to jobs held in foreign countries if applicable.

12. Since you received your first university degree *or* since you completed your education before the university level if you do not presently hold a university degree:
    (a) how many different organizations have you worked for? number _____
    (b) how many times have you changed your job? number _____
    (c) how many times have you shifted geographical locations (i.e. moved your family and/or yourself to a different city, village or country)?
                number _____

13. Question 13 asks you about your *present job*. Please begin by completing the chart below.

(a)

What is your job title? e.g. director of chemical research; highway engineer; etc.	For what organization do you work?	What kind of industry or service is this? e.g. drug mfg.; provincial road construction; etc.	Where do your work	How many hours do you work per week in this job?	How long have you held this job? (specify dates)
					FROM TO
					_____ present
			village or city		
			province or country		

(b) Please specify the monetary benefits that you have received for this job in the last year:

MONETARY BENEFIT	AMOUNT IN RIALS	TIME UNIT
Salary		per month
Living allowance		per month
Overtime		per
Bonuses		per
Special Project Pay		per
Other: specify		per

(c) Are you under a definite contract with this organization?
        Yes ☐   No ☐
(d) Were you promoted from within the organization to this job?
        No ☐   Yes ☐   (if Yes, skip to 13(f).)
(e) How did you learn about this job?
    (1) friends . . . .☐
    (2) relatives . . . .☐
    (3) ads in newspapers or journals . . . .☐
    (4) direct application to the organization . . . .☐
    (5) other: specify _____ . . . .☐
(f) Do you presently hold any other job(s) other than the one specified above, or are you self-employed in any capacity?
        Yes ☐   No ☐   (if No, skip to question 14.)
(g) If Yes, please list the details of your alternative form(s) of employment in the chart below:

What is (are) your job title(s)? 1.	Employment Status 1. Private Sector Employee 2. Gov't Employee 3. Self-employed 4. Unpaid family worker	What kind of industry or service is this?	What is the location of your work-place?	What are your average hours of work per week?	What is your average income per month? (in rials)	How long have you held the job(s)? FROM TO Present
			village or city			
			province or country			
2.						
			village or city			
			province or country			
3.						
			village or city			
			province or country			

14. Question 14 asks you about your *previous job* (i.e. the job you held before your present one). If you have had only one job since receiving your first university degree or completing your pre-university education if you have no degree, skip to Section IV.

(a) Please complete the chart below with reference to your previous job:

What was your job title?	Employment Status 1. Private Sector Employee 2. Gov't Employee 3. Self-employed 4. Unpaid family worker	What kind of industry or service was this?	What was the location of your work-place?	What was your average income per month in this job? (rials)	How long did you hold this job? (specify dates) FROM TO
			village or city		
			province or country		

(b) Were you under a definite contract with this organization?
        Yes ☐   No ☐

(c) Were you promoted from within the organization to this job?
        No ☐   Yes ☐   (If Yes, skip to 14(e).)

(d) How did you learn about this job?
   (1) friends . . . . ——
   (2) relatives . . . . ——
   (3) ads in newspapers or journals . . . . ——
   (4) direct application to the organization . . . . ——
   (5) other: specify _____ . . . . ——

(e) If this job was not with the same organization and/or in the same geographical location (i.e. village, city, province or country) as your present job, specify in detail your reasons for the job move:
   Reasons _____
   _____
   _____

15. Question 15 asks you about the first job you held after you completed your first university degree requirements or your pre-university education if you do not have a university degree. If your "first job" was the same as your "previous job", skip to Section IV.

(a) Please complete the chart below with reference to your first job:

What was your job title?	Employment Status 1. Private Sector Employee 2. Gov't Employee 3. Self-employed 4. Unpaid family worker	What kind of industry or service was this	What was the location of your work-place?	What was your average income per month in this job? (rials)	How long did you hold this job? (specify dates)
					FROM TO
			Village or City		
			Province or Country		

(b) Were you under a definite contract with this organization?
　　　　　　Yes　□　　　No　□

(c) How did you learn about this job?
　　(1) friends . . . . ._____
　　(2) relatives . . . . ._____
　　(3) ads in newspapers or journals . . . . ._____
　　(4) direct application to the organization . . . . ._____
　　(5) other: specify _____ . . . . ._____

SECTION IV: CHANGE WITHIN A GENERATION

This section asks you questions concerning your family history. It is to be answered by Iranian citizens *only*.

16. Where were you born? _____ ; _____ ; _____
　　　　　　　　　　　　　　　city or village　　　　province　　　　country

17. Where were you living when you were 18 years old?
　　　　　　　　　　　　　　　_____ ; _____ ; _____
　　　　　　　　　　　　　　　city or village　　　　province　　　　country

18. Were you living with both your parents most of the time up to age 18?
　　　　No　□　　　Yes　□　　　　　　　　　　　(If Yes, skip to question 20.)

19. If No, who was the head of your family?
　　(a) father □　　　(c) other male　□
　　(b) mother □　　　(d) other female □

20. What occupation did your father (or person indicated in question 19) have when you were 18 years old?
　　　　　　　　　　　　　　　Occupation _____

21. What kind of industry was this?
　　　　　　　　　　　　　　　Industry _____

22. Was (s)he:
　　(a) An employee for a private company, business, or individual for wages, salary, or commissions. . . . . . .□
　　(b) A government employee (Federal, State, County, or Local Government). . . . .□
　　(c) Self-employed in own business, professional practice, or farm . . . .□
　　(d) Working without pay in family's business or farm . . . .□

23. What is the educational background of your father (or person indicated in question 19)? (If you are not sure, please make a guess.)
　　(a) illiterate . . . .□
　　(b) literate but with no formal qualifications . . . .□
　　(c) literate with certificate or degree received: . . . .□
　　　　Specify highest degree or certificate
　　　　received: _____

THANK YOU FOR YOUR CO-OPERATION

BIBLIOGRAPHY

Adelman, I., and E. Thorbecke, eds. *The Theory and Design of Economic Development*. Baltimore: Johns Hopkins Press, 1966.

Amuzegar, Jahangir, and M. Ali Fekrat. *Iran: Economic Development Under Dualistic Conditions*. Chicago: University of Chicago Press, 1971.

Arasteh, Reza. *Education and Social Awakening in Iran*. Leiden: Brill, 1962.

Aresvik, Oddvar. *The Agricultural Development of Iran*. New York: Praeger, 1976.

Asadi, Hamideh, "Some Reflections on the Problem of Importing Skilled Manpower." Paper presented at joint Plan and Budget Organization and OECD meeting on Basic Issues of Iran's Long-Term Development and World Economic Trends, Tehran, September 30–October 2, 1975. Mimeographed.

Ashraf, Ahmad Ervand. "Historical Obstacles to the Development of a Bourgeoisie in Iran." *Iranian Studies* 2 (1969): 54–79.

Avery, Peter. *Modern Iran*. London: Ernest Benn, 1965.

Baldwin, George B. "Four Studies on the Iranian Brain Drain." In The Committee on the International Migration of Talent, *The International Migration of High-Level Manpower, Its Impact on the Development Process*, pp. 374–96. New York: Praeger, 1970.

——. *Planning and Development in Iran*. Baltimore: Johns Hopkins Press, 1967.

——. "The Foreign-Educated Iranian: A Profile." *Middle East Journal* 17 (Summer, 1963): 264–278.

Bank Markazi Iran. *Survey of Selected Manufacturing Industries in 1353* (1974/75). Tehran, 1975.

Bartsch, William H. *Problems of Employment Creation in Iran*. Geneva: International Labor Organization, 1970.

Basu, S. K., S. Ghosh, and R. N. Banerjee. *Labour Market Behaviour in a Developing Economy*. New Dehli: New Age, 1969.

Becker, Gary. *Human Capital*. New York: National Bureau of Economic Research, 1964.

Becker, H. S., and A. Strauss. "Careers, Personality and Adult Socialization." *American Journal of Sociology* 62 (November, 1956): 253–63.

Bhalla, A. S., ed. *Technology and Employment in Industry: A Case Study Approach*. Geneva: International Labor Organization, 1975.

111

Bharier, J. *Economic Development in Iran: 1900-1970.* New York: Oxford University Press, 1971.

Bill, James A. "Class Analysis and the Dialectics of Modernization in the Middle East." *International Journal of Middle East Studies* 3 (1972): 417-434.

——. *The Politics of Iran: Groups, Classes and Modernization.* Columbus, Ohio: Merrill, 1972.

——. "The Plasticity of Informal Politics: The Case of Iran." Paper delivered at the Conference on the Structure of Power in Islamic Iran, University of California, Los Angeles, June 1969.

——. "The Social and Economic Foundations of Power in Iran." *Middle East Journal* 17 (Autumn 1963): 400-418.

Binder, Leonard. *Iran: Political Development in a Changing Society.* Berkeley: University of California Press, 1962.

——. "The Cabinet of Iran: A Case Study in Institutional Adaptation." *Middle East Journal* 16 (Winter 1962): 29-47.

Blau, Peter M. *The Dynamics of Bureaucracy.* Chicago: University of Chicago Press, 1955.

Blau, Peter M., and Otis D. Duncan. *The American Occupational Structure.* New York: Wiley, 1967.

Blaug, Mark. "The Correlation Between Education and Earnings: What Does It Signify?" *Higher Education* 3 (Winter, 1972): 53-76.

——. *The Utilisation of Educated Manpower in Industry: A Preliminary Report.* London: Oliver and Boyd, 1967.

Blaug, Mark, M. Peston, and A. Ziderman. "Efficiency and the Labour Force." *New Education*, September 1966.

Bottomore, T. B. *Classes in Modern Society.* New York: Basic Books, 1962.

Caplow, T. *Principles of Organization.* New York: Harcourt, Brace and World, 1964.

——. *The Sociology of Work.* New York: McGraw-Hill, 1954.

Carey, J. P. C., and A. G. Carey. "Industrial Growth and Development Planning in Iran." *Middle East Journal* 29 (Winter 1975): 1-15.

Central Treaty Organization. *Seminar in Industrial Relations.* Tehran, 1972.

Chenery, H. B., ed. *Studies in Development Planning.* Cambridge, Mass.: Harvard University Press, 1971.

Cox, T. Hillard. "High-Level Manpower Development in Iran." Study prepared for Governmental Affairs Institute, Tehran, 1960. Mimeographed.

Davidson, P. E., and D. Anderson. *Occupational Mobility in an American Community* Palo Alto, Calif.: Stanford University Press, 1937.

de Girvy, J., and J. Scoville. "Labour Legislation: Practice and Theory." Working paper no. 9 prepared for *Employment and Income Policies in Iran*. Geneva: International Labor Organization, 1973.

DePasquale, J. A., and R. A. Lange. "Job Hopping in the MBA." *Harvard Business Review* 49 (November–December, 1971): 11–12, 151–154.

Doeringer, Peter B., and Michael J. Piore. *International Labor Markets and Manpower Analysis.* Lexington, Mass.: Heath, 1971.

Fesharaki, Fereidun. *The Development of the Iranian Oil Industry.* New York: Praeger, 1976.

Firoozi, Ferydoon. "Demographic Review–Iranian Censuses 1956 and 1966: A Comparative Analysis." *Middle East Journal* 24 (Spring 1970): 220–28.

Hessam-Vaziri, A. *Report on the Study of Young Iranian Workers Problems of Adaptation to Modernization.* Tehran: Institute for Research and Planning in Science and Education, 1970.

Gable, R. W., "Culture and Administration in Iran." *Middle East Journal* 13 (1959): 407–21.

Galbraith, John K. *The New Industrial State.* Boston: Houghton Mifflin, 1967.

Gastil, Raymond G. "Middle Class Impediments to Iranian Modernization." *Public Opinion Quarterly* 22 (Fall 1958): 325–29.

Gerschendron, Alexander. *Economic Backwardness in Historical Perspective.* Cambridge, Mass.: Harvard University Press, 1962.

Gitelman, H. M. "Occupational Mobility Within the Firm." *Industrial and Labor Relations Review* 20 (October 1966): 50–65.

Goitein, S. D. *Studies in Islamic History and Institutions.* Leiden: Brill, 1966.

Graham, Robert. *Iran: The Illusion of Power.* New York: St. Martin's Press, 1978.

Gupta, P. S. "The Problem of Employment and Unemployment in Iran." Working paper no. 1 prepared for *Employment and Income Policies*. Geneva: International Labor Organization, 1973.

Hall, Richard H. *Occupations and the Social Structure.* Englewood Cliffs, N.J.: Prentice-Hall, 1969.

Halliday, Fred. *Iran: Dictatorship and Development.* London: Penguin, 1979.

Halpern, Manfred. *The Politics of Social Change in the Middle East and North Africa.* Princeton, N.J.: Princeton University Press, 1963.

Hirschman, Albert O. *The Strategy of Economic Development.* New Haven, Conn.: Yale University Press, 1958.

Institute for Research and Planning in Science and Education. *Statistics of Higher Education in Iran.* Tehran, 1976.

International Labor Organization. *International Standard Classification of Occupations.* Rev. ed. Geneva, 1975.

——. *Employment and Income Policies in Iran.* Geneva, 1973.

——. "Evolution of Labor Legislation and Administration in Iran." *International Labor Review* 69 (March 1959): 273-95.

International Monetary Fund. *International Financial Statistics,* January 1959.

Iran Almanac: 1976, 15th ed. Tehran: Echo of Iran Press, 1966.

Iran Almanac: 1966, 5th ed. Tehran: Echo of Iran Press, 1966.

Iran: Who's Who: 1976. Tehran: Echo of Iran Press, 1976.

Jacobs, Norman. *The Sociology of Development: Iran as an Asian Case Study.* New York: Praeger, 1966.

Jacqz, Jane, ed. *Iran: Past, Present and Future: The Persepolis Symposium.* New York: Aspen Institute for Humanistic Studies, 1976.

Johnson, Gail Cook. "Institutional Processes Determining the Behavior of High-Level Manpower in Iran." Ph.D. dissertation, Massachusetts Institute of Technology, 1978.

Johnson, John J. *Continuity in Latin America.* Stanford, Calif.: Stanford University Press, 1968.

Kayhan Research Associates. *Share Participation.* Tehran, 1976.

Keddie, Nikki R. "The Iranian Power Structure and Social Change, 1800-1969: An Overview." *International Journal of Middle East Studies* 2 (January 1971): 3-20.

Kerr, Clark, John T. Dunlop, Frederick Harbison, and Charles A. Myers. *Industrialism and Industrial Man.* Cambridge, Mass.: Harvard University Press, 1960.

Kindleberger, Charles. *Economic Growth in France and Britain, 1850-1950.* Cambridge, Mass.: Harvard University Press, 1964.

Krause, Elliot A. *The Sociology of Occupations.* Boston: Little, Brown, 1971.

Lambton, Ann. *The Persian Land Reform 1962-1966.* London: Oxford University Press, 1969.

Laqueur, Walter Z., ed. *The Middle East in Transition: Studies in Contemporary History.* New York: Praeger, 1958.

Lauterback, Albert. *Enterprise in Latin America.* Ithaca, N.Y.: Cornell University Press, 1966.

Layard, P. R. G., J. D. Sargan, M. E. Ager, and D. J. Jones. *Qualified Manpower and Economic Performance.* London: Allen Lane, Penguin, 1971.

Leff, Nathaniel H. "Industrial Organization and Entrepreneurship in the Developing Countries: The Economic Groups." *Economic Development and Cultural Change* 26 (July 1978): 661–75.

Levy, Reuben. *The Social Structure of Iran.* Cambridge: Cambridge University Press, 1962.

Lipset, Seymour Martin, and Aldo Solari, eds. *Elite in Latin America.* New York: Oxford University Press, 1969.

Looney, Robert E. *A Development Strategy for Iran Through the 1980s.* New York: Praeger, 1977.

Mabro, R. "Industry." Working paper no. 5 prepared for *Employment and Income Policies in Iran.* Geneva: International Labor Organization, 1973.

Madras State Employment Information Unit. *Short-Term Study of the Utilisation of Educated Persons Produced During the Third Plan Period in Madras State.* Madras, 1968.

Makler, Harry M. "Labor Problems of Native, Migrant and Foreign-Born Members of the Recife Industrial Elite." *Journal of Developing Areas.* (October 1974): 27–51.

Miller, William Green. "Political Organization in Iran: From Dowreh to Political Party." *Middle East Journal* 23 (Spring 1969, Summer 1969): 159–67, 343–50.

Millward, William G. "Traditional Values and Social Change in Iran." *Iranian Studies* 4 (Winter 1971): 2–35.

Ministry of Economy, Iran. *1968 Industrial Statistics.* Tehran, 1968.

Ministry of Industry and Mines, Iran. *Iranian Industrial Statistics, 1972.* Tehran, 1974.

Ministry of Labour and Social Affairs, Iran. *Results of the Manpower Survey, 1972.* Tehran, 1974.

——. *Household Sample Survey, December 1969–January 1970.* Tehran, 1972.

——. *Household Sample Survey, May–June, 1969.* Tehran: 1972.

Nie, N. H., C. H. Hall, J. G. Jenkins, K. Steinberger, and D. H. Brent. *Statistical Package for the Social Sciences.* 2nd ed. New York: McGraw-Hill, 1975.

Nieuwenhuijze, C. A. O. van. *Social Stratification and the Middle East, An Interpretation.* Leiden: Brill, 1965.

Organization for Economic Cooperation and Development. *The Utilisation of Highly Qualified Manpower: Venice Conference: 25th–27th October 1971.* Paris, 1973.

Oshima, H. "Income Distribution." Working paper no. 2 prepared for *Employment and Income Policies in Iran*. Geneva: International Labor Organization, 1973.

Pahlavi, Mohammed Reza Shah. *Mission for My Country*. London: Hutchinson, 1974.

Parsons, Talcott. "Pattern Variables Revisited." *American Sociological Review* 25 (August 1960): 467–83.

——. *The Social System*. Glencoe, Ill.: Free Press, 1951.

Patchen, M. *The Choice of Wage Comparisons*. Englewood Cliffs, N.J.: Prentice-Hall, 1961.

Plan and Budget Organization, Iran. *Summary of the Fifth National Plan, 1973–1978*. Tehran, 1974.

Psacharopoulos, G., and G. Williams. "Education and Vocational Training." Working paper no. 8 prepared for *Employment and Income Policies in Iran*. Geneva: International Labor Organization, 1973.

Ramazani, R. K. "'Church' and State in Modernizing Society: The Case of Iran." *American Behavioral Scientist* 7 (January 1964): 26–28.

——. "Modernization and Social Research in Iran." *American Behavioral Scientist* 5 (1962): 17–20.

Reder, M. "Wage Structure: Theory and Measurement." In *Aspects of Labor Economics*. Princeton, N.J.: Princeton University Press for National Bureau of Economic Research, 1962, pp. 257–311.

Richardson, G. B. "Organization of Industry." *Economic Journal* September 1972, pp. 883–96.

Richardson, Olga. "Industrial Licensing." Tehran: Iran Centre for Management Studies, 1976. Mimeographed.

Richardson, Peter. "Business Policy in Iran." *Journal of General Management*, forthcoming.

Rostow, W. W. *The Stages of Economic Growth*. Cambridge: Cambridge University Press, 1960.

Srivastava, R. K. "A Preliminary Review of the Employment and Manpower Situation in Iran." Working paper prepared for the ILO Manpower Project in conjunction with the Plan and Budget Organization, Tehran, 1975. Mimeographed.

Starbuck, W. H., ed. *Organizational Growth and Development*. London: Penguin, 1971.

Statistical Centre of Iran. *National Census of Population and Housing, 1966*. Tehran, 1968.

——. *National Census of Population and Housing, 1956*. Tehran, 1958.

Tarrant, John L. "Worldwide Variations in Management Style." *Management Review*, April 1976, pp. 36–39.

Timmer, Peter C., et al. *The Choice of Technology in Developing Countires.* Cambridge, Mass.: Harvard University Press, 1975.

UNESCO. *The International Classification of Education.* Abridged ed. Paris, 1975.

Vakil, Firouz. "Iran's Basic Macroeconomic Problems: A 20-Year Horizon." *Economic Development and Cultural Change* 25 (July 1977): 713-29.

Westwood, Andrew F. "Politics of Distrust in Iran." *Annals of the American Academy of Political and Social Science* 358 (March 1965): 397-415.

——. "Elections and Politics in Iran." *Middle East Journal* 15 (Spring 1961): 153-64.

Wheeler, A. C. R. "The Development of Industrial Employment in Iran Before 1353 (1974/ 75)." Working paper prepared for ILO Manpower Project in conjunction with Plan and Budget Organization, Tehran, 1976.

——. "Industrial Surveys in Iran." Working paper prepared for the ILO Manpower Project in conjunction with the Plan and Budget Organization, Tehran, 1976.

White, Lawrence J. "The Evidence on Appropriate Factor Proportions for Manufacturing in Less Developed Countries: A Survey." *Economic Development and Cultural Change* 27 (October 1978): 27-59.

Wilensky, Harold. "Orderly Careers and Social Participation." *American Sociological Review* (August 1961): 521-39.

Williamson, Oliver E. "The Vertical Integration of Production: Market Failure Considerations." *American Economic Review* (May 1971): 112-23.

Woodward, Joan. *Industrial Organization: Theory and Practice.* London: Oxford University Press, 1966.

Yar-Shater, E., ed. *Iran Faces the 1970s.* New York: Praeger, 1971.

Zonis, Marvin. *The Political Elite of Iran.* Princeton, N.J.: Princeton University Press, 1976.

Zonoosi, A., and H. Khazaneh. *Investigation into Statistic Sources of Manpower in the Country.* Translated by Jaleh Basseri. Tehran: College of Translation, 1974.

INDEX

agriculture, poor performance of 13; percentage of labor force 96
anti-profiteering, (see) legal policies: anti-profiteering regulations
Amouzegar, Iamshed 27
Amuzegar, Jahangir and Fekrat, M. Ali 12
Armenians 80
auto industry 15, 33, 44
Ayandegan 62

backward integration, in industrialization policy 18, (see also) vertical integration
Bahai 81
Bank Markazi (Central Bank of Iran) 14, 15, 26
Bank Omran 30
banks, ownership by companies 46; manpower in 62
bazaar merchants 47
Bazargan, Mehdi 103
benefits, monetary for HLM, (see) remuneration
Bill, James 79, 81, 85, 86
black market in cars 33
Blau, Peter 59, and Otis Duncan 71, 78, 73-76
brain drain 18
brick-making industry 15
budget, government overruns 27
bureaucracy, government, (see) public sector

Cabinet 26
capacity utilization 15
career profiles 80-87
career success, determinants of 71-80
cement industry 15
Central Bank of Iran, (see) Bank Markazi
centralization, of Shah's authority 26-27; of decision making in organizations 48-51, 60-61; in Tehran 25-26
civil service, (see) public sector
collective bargaining 35
communications, in organization 49
computers 51
Congress of Workers 28

connections, importance of for career success 78, 84-85
consultants, public sector 62-63
costs, of production 47
Council for the Expansion of Public Ownership of Productive Units 26
credentialism, in labor market 85, 92

decision-making in organizations 48-49
deficit, government 11
dismissals, cost of 35, 56
Dispute Settlement Board 35
Duncan, Otis and Peter Blau 71, 73-76, 78

economic development, (see) industrialization
education, impact of father's on child's 73; impact on career 73, 77, 78-80, 86; (see also) institutions of higher education
Elghanian, Habib 81
elite 86
empire building, fear of in organizations 49, 61
employment, in industry 15-17; in public sector 18; in agriculture 96
entrepreneurs, flight of 31, 35; capabilities of 38, 43, 92; attitudes of 43; background of 47; decision-making authority of 48-49
Eqbal, Dr. Manouchehr 38n1
ethnic minorities 80-82; (see also) outer fringe
expectations gap 3
exporter, Iranian hopes as major 15, 47
exports 31; (see also) legal policies: import-export laws
extended kinship system 48

Fekrat, M. Ali and Amuzegar, Jahangir 12
field of study, impact on career 19, 83, 87
Fifth Plan 11, 12-14, 25, 26-27
Followers 85-86
foreign nationals, number of 16; attitude toward 16-17, 63; as managers in multinational case 48, 100; careers of 80-81; salaries of 89-90; under

ABOUT THE AUTHOR

GAIL COOK JOHNSON presently is completing a study of high-level manpower for the Ontario government in Canada and teaches part-time at the University of Toronto.

Before returning to Canada, Dr. Johnson lived in Iran and conducted the research which is the subject of her dissertation entitled "Institutional Processes Governing the Behaviour of High-Level Manpower in Iran." This work laid the foundations for this present book. Dr. Johnson received her Ph.D. from the Sloan School of Management, Massachusetts Institute of Technology.